KT-428-277

EAST SUSSEX COUNTY COUNCIL
WITHDRAWN
2 1 JUN 2024
20

04242230

The Naughtiest
VEGAN CAKES
in Town

For Jamie and Gareth – for giving
meaning to everything in my life

The Naughtiest VEGAN CAKES in Town

MELLISSA MORGAN

◨ SQUARE PEG

LONDON

CONTENTS

Ms. Cupcake THE BEGINNING

Ms. Cupcake was born back in 2009 in the lil' ol' kitchen of my tiny two-bed flat in South London. You see, when I was making the leap from vegetarianism to veganism, I had a good look around London but couldn't find the cake I wanted to eat. I wanted decadent, indulgent, celebrate-your-belly kind of cake – that also happened to be vegan. At that time, no one in the UK was doing what North America had long cottoned on to – across the pond there's a vegan bakery in every big city! Not being the type to weep into my mixing bowl, I pulled on my apron and got baking. I had never worked in the food industry, nor had I ever run my own business, but what I did have going for me was a ridiculous amount of determination and a desire to show the world that indulgence and veganism can work together.

It was a cold day at the beginning of April 2010 when Mamma-Cupcake (my mum actually flew over from Canada for the start of it all) and I set up my first market stall in Greenwich Market. I think I sold 36 cupcakes that day, and my goodness was I on top of the world! I don't pretend that I knew what the heck I was doing in those early days, but I was willing to graft and learn. I was quite a sight on the market stall – a nutty Canadian gal dressed as a 1950s housewife with a hat adorned with cupcakes – and within a few months word had spread (partially through the glory of social media) and people were queuing up for the decadent 'free-from' cakes they'd been hearing about.

I began to get asked about providing bakes for even more diets, so I set about broadening my range to include gluten-free, soya-free and pretty much anything-free you can think of! Back then I was pulling 18-hour days, 7 days a week and crawling into bed absolutely exhausted each night. I hired staff and had friends pitch in (thanks Liz!), but something had to give. I needed guidance. So I closed my market stall for a couple of weeks and boarded a plane to the east coast of America, to talk to other vegan bakers and find out how they made it all work for them. Meeting Barbara from Gone Pie, Heather and Allison from Sweet Freedom and the beautiful Danielle, Jake, Kristina and Ann over at Sweet Avenue Bakery made me realise, 'If they can do it, so can I!'

Every penny we made from cupcakes in those early days we reinvested in the business, and I am proud to say that on 1 April 2011 we opened the doors to London's first entirely vegan retail bakery, Ms. Cupcake, in Brixton, on my home turf in South London. My choice of location may have raised a few eyebrows, but I didn't care. I love Brixton. I love the people, the vibe and the passion of the area. I figured if people wanted to buy vegan cake, they'd have to come down to Brixton and maybe fall in love with it too. Besides, if you don't help your local community to grow, who will?

Our mission at Ms. Cupcake is to make cakes you'd never know were vegan. I want our cakes to be considered just as good, or even better, than cakes made with traditional ingredients. A few weeks after we opened, one of our regular customers, who had been buying our cakes since our very first day, asked us, 'So what is this "vegan" you put in all of your cakes?' Brilliant, I thought, mission accomplished!

My staff are the cornerstone of our success. Hand-picked from all over the world, they are the most passionate and committed people I know. Without their dedication and love, our customers wouldn't keep coming back.

We all work incredibly hard, but we wouldn't have it any other way. We believe that everybody deserves great cake and it is our job to create indulgent and decadent cakes for them regardless of what they can, and cannot, eat. Every time a mum brings in her child, who is battling serious allergies, and tells them, 'You can eat anything here, it's all safe.' I can't help but well up. This is why we do what we do! Help us to continue to spread the love by baking up a vegan storm and sharing your results with your friends and family.

After all, everyone deserves great cake.

Vegan Baking THE QUICK-START GUIDE

I never read the introductions to cookbooks, so well done for reading mine! Whenever I get my mitts on a new book I just want to get into the kitchen and get on to the good stuff – the baking! However, if you have never baked a vegan cake before or have had less-than-perfect results, have a gander over this and you'll be fully equipped for vegan baking success! Take time to read the tips, tricks and knowledge sprinkled throughout the book. You'll find some real gems discovered by us over all the years we've spent creating unconventional bakes. These tips might just transform your cake from 'okay' to 'spectacular'.

Vegan Baking WHAT'S MISSING?

Nowadays you can get a hold of loads of dairy replacements or 'plant-based milks' at your local supermarket. These include:

SOYA MILK

RICE MILK

OAT MILK

COCONUT MILK

NUT MILKS (ALMOND, HAZELNUT ETC.)

The list goes on. Soya is the most versatile of milks and the one that we use the most. It has great binding properties that help hold the cake together, but it is an allergen and some people prefer to avoid it in their diets. Our next favourite is rice milk. Its flavour won't come through in your baking so the other ingredients can do the singing. Rice milk does give cakes a slightly different texture than soya and you may find a few tiny holes, or air pockets, in the sponge. Do play around with different milks until you get the results you are after. We tend to use the unsweetened varieties, but sweetened versions will do in a pinch.

Manufacturers in the UK have realised there is huge potential for growth in the 'free-from' market, so there are plenty of non-dairy margarines out there. Check the packaging to make sure there is no 'whey' in them, as this is a dairy derivative. Non-dairy margarines have a more fragile structure than butter, so you may need to include a vegetable fat or 'shortening' in the recipe to get the right texture. These are also readily available – have a look in the butter aisle of your local supermarket.

People ask us all the time, 'What do you use instead of eggs?' In baking, eggs act both as a raising agent and as a binder, but there are plenty of other ingredients you can use instead. For raising, we use bicarbonate of soda (baking soda) and baking powder. For binding, we find different ingredients work for different bakes. Here's an easy guide:

NOTHING In some recipes, such as sponge cakes, you don't actually need anything to replace the egg. Just be careful not to overmix the wet batter or you'll end up with a dense sponge. It's important to work quickly and get the batter in the oven straightaway so that the raising agents don't have time to start working before they are in the oven.

CURDLED SOYA MILK By adding cider vinegar or lemon juice to soya milk you can create a great alternative to buttermilk. For every 100ml (just under ½ a cup) of soya milk, add about 10ml (2 teaspoons) of vinegar. This method is perfect for light sponges and cupcakes.

FRUIT OR VEGETABLE PURÉES Puréed apple, pear, pumpkin and banana help to bind sweet batters, loaf cakes and muffins brilliantly. About 30–40g (¼ cup) of purée is the equivalent of one medium-sized egg. Remember that the flavour of the fruit or vegetable will be noticeable in your bake, so choose accordingly!

SILKEN TOFU You can use tofu in a similar way to fruit and vegetable purées, but we don't use this ingredient very often as it can make the bake quite dense and heavy. Try it with something like brownies, where denseness is what you are looking for.

SOYA OR COCONUT YOGHURT This works better than tofu in vegan bakes. We blend it into batters and fried treats and it also works well in loaf cakes and muffins. Use about 30–50g (¼–⅓ cup) for each egg you need to replace.

GROUND FLAXSEED This is also known as ground linseed. Mix 1 tablespoon of ground flaxseed with 3 tablespoons of water and leave to sit for a few minutes. It will turn gloopy like egg white. Ideal used in traybakes, like brownies, it will also give the top of your bake a nice crackly texture. Flaxseed does not dissolve, so you will still be able to see brown flecks of seed in your baking. We only use this in chocolate-based bakes as the colour cleverly hides the flax!

COMMERCIAL EGG REPLACEMENT PRODUCTS These shop-bought products are used to replace eggs in baking and consist of different starches that you mix with water. The result is a mixture similar to whisked egg white. As it's a bit pricey, we try not to use it in many of our cakes but find it creates awesome cookies that are crisp on the outside and chewy on the inside. All of the different brands will have directions for use on the box, but feel free to play around!

Things THAT YOU MAY want TO DO WITHOUT

Allergies and intolerances to wheat and gluten are becoming an increasing concern for many people. Thankfully there are easy-to-find pre-blended alternatives out there now which include rice, maize, potato, buckwheat and so on. When using gluten-free flour, use like-for-like measurements, but be prepared for slightly different results to those you would get using wheat flour. You will also find that vegan gluten-free bakes do not have a very long shelf life and most are best consumed within 48 hours.

We *love* sugar at Ms. Cupcake. When I first went vegan I was surprised to find that not all sugar is vegan-friendly as it is sometimes refined using charred animal bones (yikes!) Although all sugar produced in the UK is entirely vegan-friendly, those living in the US, Canada and other parts of the world will need to source a 'vegan sugar' (see Stockists and Suppliers list on page 152). If you don't like using sugar at all, try replacing it with:

AGAVE NECTAR This is a liquid sweetener which comes from a cactus-like plant called the 'agave'. It is similar to honey in consistency and sweetness.

RICE SYRUP Made from rice, this has a texture akin to honey or molasses. Rice syrup has a smilar number of calories to other liquid sweeteners and is not a suitable alternative for diabetics. Occasionally rice syrup contains gluten, so check the label if you are intolerant.

XYLITOL A sugar substitute that can be purchased in a crystallised form and is similar in texture to granulated sugar. Xylitol has a very low GI (glycaemic index) level which makes it easy to metabolise and therefore ideal for diabetics and those with hyperglycaemia. Unfortunately it is much more expensive than sugar.

STEVIA A no-calorie plant-derived sweetener that is 300 times sweeter than sugar in its natural form. It has only recently been licensed for food consumption in the EU, but there are currently many different brands available. Stevia powder is best avoided in baking, however, as it is a tricky beast to use. Opt instead for commercially made stevia sugar-replacement brands that have been created to replicate sugar's texture.

DATE SYRUP This syrup is derived entirely from dates and will add a rich and intense flavour to your bakes. It has a similar consistency to treacle or molasses and is great used in its raw form, drizzled over dairy-free ice creams, yoghurts or other desserts. It is not a suitable alternative for diabetics.

MAPLE SYRUP Made from the sap of maple trees, this syrup has a distinct flavour which comes through in your baking. Maple syrup has significantly risen in price over the last few years, so you might like to try one of the maple-flavoured syrups on the market. These are considerably cheaper but have a milder taste.

Not all of these alternative ingredients can be swapped like-for-like in recipes, so you will need to play around with quantities until you get them right. Note that syrup products will have a much higher burn rate, so you'll need to bake at a lower temperature for a bit longer.

Ms. Cupcake's RULES FOR Vegan Baking

Some of the methods in this book you may find odd or unconventional if you are unfamiliar with vegan baking. However, I cannot stress enough how important it is to follow our directions so that you get the right results.

HERE ARE A FEW Guidelines

★★★ DON'T STIR TOO MUCH ★★★

When we say, 'stir until just combined', we mean it! If you stir for a long time or (God forbid) put your cake batter in an electric mixer, you will be asking for a dense, thick cake! Excessive stirring overworks the gluten in the flour and without the eggs to help leaven the batter the result will be a cake that is dense and flat. Forget what you know about 'whipping air into the batter to make it light and fluffy', this will not work with vegan baking!

★★★ TAP, TAP, TAP ★★★

We're serious when we say we don't want the raising agents to work until they're in the oven! We always 'tap out the bubbles' before placing any bake in the oven. This is especially true for cupcakes and layer cakes, where you can actually see the air bubbles forming on the top of the wet cake batter. Give the mixing bowl a whack on the counter before putting the batter in your tray, then give the tray another whack before it hits the oven shelf. We also tap our cookie trays when they come *out* of the oven. This is to flatten out the cookies so that they aren't too dense. Alternatively, you can press the cookies with a spatula, but the tapping method is less messy.

★★★ KEEP AN EYE ON THE SHELF LIFE ★★★ OF YOUR BAKES

Vegan cakes tend to have a shorter shelf life than non-vegan ones. This isn't usually a problem as they are so scrummy they are eaten straight away! However, if you want to keep your cakes for a few days, unless the recipe says otherwise, store everything at room temperature. Keeping cookies, cakes and cupcakes in the fridge dries them out and they will become stale much quicker. You can, however, freeze pretty much everything in the book for up to 3 months, so if you want to pace yourself, cut your bake into portion sizes and freeze them individually, then just defrost as needed. If you are using gluten- and wheat-free flours, the shelf life of your bakes will be even shorter, I'm afraid (they're best consumed within 48 hours). Play around with the recipe and try adding some fruit purées or more oil to your bake to see if that improves its shelf life before it hits your belly.

★★★ AS SOON AS THE LIQUID HITS, ACT FAST! ★★★

In most of our recipes we mix the dry ingredients first and then add in the wet ones. It is really important not to dawdle once the wet mixture hits the dry. Baking powder starts working the second it comes into contact with liquid, so don't let your batter hang about. You want the raising action to happen inside the oven, not while the bowl is sitting on the counter. In traditional baking, this is less of a problem as egg is such a forgiving ingredient, but in vegan baking it results in a gooey, dense mess.

★★★ DON'T DECORATE OR EAT YOUR BAKE ★★★ STRAIGHT AWAY – LET IT REST

When I discovered this tip a couple of years ago, I was surprised more people don't do it. After you bake a cake or a cupcake it will often have a thin 'crust' on the top and sides of the bake. You can eliminate this crispness by putting your cooled bake into an airtight plastic container for a couple of hours or overnight. The moisture of the cake will work its way through the cake and you will be left with a very soft sponge. Just ensure that it is completely cooled before sealing it, as a warm cake will create condensation and you will end up with a wet cake instead of a moist one.

COMMON Vegan Baking PROBLEMS

No matter how hard you try, sometimes it all goes wrong. Here are some common problems found in vegan baking and possible explanations.

★★★ MY CAKES ARE NOT RISING ★★★

Are you tapping? (See our tip on page 11.) If you are, and your bakes are still not rising, double-check that you are using the correct quantities of all your ingredients, especially the wet ones, as it could be there is too much moisture in your mix. Also check the temperature inside your oven using an oven thermometer. If the oven isn't hot enough your cake won't rise correctly. Finally, make sure your baking powder is fresh and in date.

★★★ MY CAKES RISE IN THE OVEN, BUT SAG ★★★ IN THE MIDDLE WHEN I TAKE THEM OUT

This is usually caused by your baking powder. Not all baking powders are created equal, and different brands have different strengths. This is also true of self-raising flour, which varies from brand to brand. If you find your cakes drop after rising it usually means you are adding *too much* baking powder. Surprised? Trust me – try the recipe with less and you'll get better results.

★★★ MY COOKIES ARE NOT SPREADING, ★★★ OR THEY ARE SPREADING TOO MUCH

This could be due to the fat content of your cookies. If you want your cookies to spread out more when baking, add 10–20 grams (2–4 teaspoons) more margarine or vegetable fat (shortening) to the recipe. If they are spreading out too much, try reducing the fat content. Alternatively, refrigerate the dough first so it is cold when it goes in the oven. Failing that, adjust your oven temperature either up or down a few degrees to see if this does the trick.

★★★ MY CUPCAKE CASES ARE PEELING ★★★ AWAY FROM MY CUPCAKES

This is a common complaint so don't be surprised if this happens to you. Cupcake cases come in different thicknesses and we find that the thicker cases are almost always the ones that pull away, Expensive cupcake cases tend to have thicker paper so choose a cheaper case and it is more likely to stay in place. Tapping, or banging, your tray on the counter before baking also helps to keep the cases in place as it eliminates air pockets between them and the batter. Finally make sure you transfer your cupcakes from the tray to wire racks to cool completely. This will prevent condensation forming which encourages the papers to peel away.

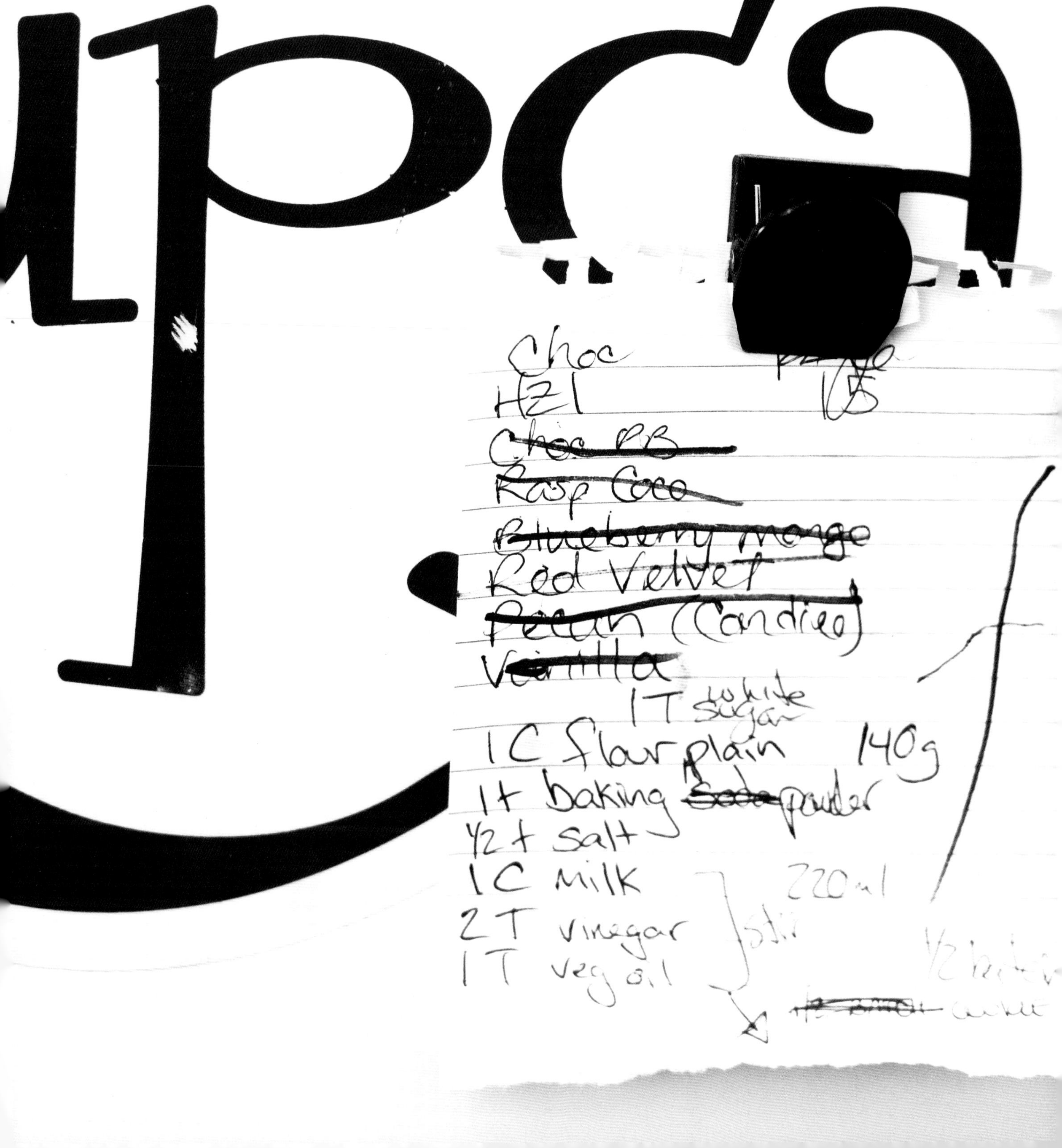

Choc

HZl

~~Choc PB~~

~~Rasp Coco~~

~~Blueberry Mange~~

~~Red Velvet~~

~~Pecan (Candied)~~

~~Vanilla~~

1T white sugar

1C flour plain   140g

1t baking ~~Soda~~ powder

1/2 t salt

1C milk   220ml

2T vinegar   } stir

1T veg oil

US vs. UK

So far, vegan baking books have been written mostly by North American authors. As a dual passport holder I get asked to translate American recipes for British cooking quite a bit, so I figured I would include these tables for some of the ingredients included in this book. Please note that these are not always direct translations! Some ingredients you can find in Britain but not in America and vice versa. In these cases, I have chosen the nearest substitute.

INGREDIENTS:

British TERM	American TERM
bicarbonate of soda	baking soda
caster sugar	granulated sugar
cornflour	corn starch
desiccated coconut	grated, flaked or shredded coconut
digestive biscuits*	no-honey graham crackers*
flaked almonds	slivered or sliced almonds
glacé cherries*	candied cherries*
golden syrup	corn syrup (but golden syrup is much better!)
vegetable fat (vegetable shortening)	shortening
icing	frosting
icing sugar	powdered sugar or confectioner's sugar*
jelly*	gelatine-free jello
plain chocolate*	semi-sweet chocolate*
plain flour	all-purpose flour
rapeseed oil	canola oil
rich tea biscuits*	animal crackers*
self-raising flour	self-rising flour
soya milk	soy milk

* These items are not always vegan, so check each brand for 'hidden' ingredients.

BRANDS:

Some American books refer to specific vegan brands for products. Here is a list of British equivalents. For ordering information, have a look at our UK Stockists and Suppliers (see page 152) at the back of the book.

Ingredient	British BRAND	American BRAND
food colouring	Squires, Sugarcraft	Wilton
margarine	Pure, Vitalite	Earth Balance
marshmallows	Sweet Vegan	Sweet and Sara, Dandies
puff pastry	Jus-Rol	Pepperidge Farms
shortening/ vegetable fat	Trex	Crisco or Earth Balance
sugar	all British sugars are vegan	Wholesome Foods, Florida Crystals, Hain Organic Powdered Sugar, Jack Frost, Country Cane, Supreme, Southern Bell, 365 (Whole Foods own brand).
chocolate	Plamil, Moo Free, Organica, Organic Seed and Bean Company	Go Max Go, Trader Joe and Whole Foods own brands, Sunspire, Tropical Source

CUPCAKES and MUFFINS

Every year we're told that cupcakes are passé but every year they seem to grow more popular. Cupcakes are here to stay my friends! They offer an incredible way for you to unleash your creative soul and are a perfect, individual gift of love for someone, or for yourself. A slice of cake is a great thing, but a cupcake is an occasion.

Our recipes are so quick and simple that they are ideal for the novice or the mum baking at home with her kids. The method is pretty much the same for all the recipes, it's the ingredients that differ, so if you can master one of the recipes, you can master them all! Just remember to mix all of the dry ingredients first before you add the wet ingredients, and get that batter into the oven quick! It will ensure that you have a beautifully risen, light and delicate sponge, every single time.

Finally, there is no right or wrong way to decorate – just do like we do, and do it with love.

wow!

BASIC *Vanilla* CUPCAKE

ADD CRUSHED VEGAN BOURBON BISCUITS TO THE VANILLA ICING AND USE TO TOP YOUR CHOCOLATE CUPCAKE. VOILA! COOKIES 'N' CREAM CUPCAKES.

New vegan bakers often ask me what recipe they should try first. My answer is always, cupcakes! The great Isa Chandra Moskowitz and Terry Hope Romero brought vegan cupcakes into the mainstream with their incredible book *Vegan Cupcakes Take Over the World* and that's exactly what got my tushie into the kitchen a few years back. Here are our simple versions of two classic flavours. Go on and get baking – these recipes are so simple you've got no excuses!

MAKES 12 LARGE CUPCAKES, 24 FAIRY CAKES OR 48 MINI CUPCAKES

200ml (¾ cup + 1 tbsp) soya milk
20ml (4 tsp) cider vinegar

GLUTEN-FREE? Substitute the traditional flour for a gluten-free flour blend plus ¼ teaspoon xanthan gum.

200g (1¾ cups) self-raising flour
200g (1 cup) caster sugar
¼ tsp salt
¼ tsp bicarbonate of soda

¼ tsp baking powder
80ml (⅓ cup) light rapeseed or other flavourless oil
1 tbsp vanilla extract or essence

FOR THE FINISHING TOUCHES

1 x quantity Vanilla Buttercream Icing (see page 54)
vegan chocolate pieces or sprinkles

Preheat the oven to 180°C/350°F/gas 4 and line your muffin tray with muffin cases.

In a small bowl, mix the soya milk and vinegar together. Set aside for 10 minutes.

In a large bowl mix the dry ingredients together by hand until fully combined. Add the soya milk mixture, the oil and the vanilla and, using a metal spoon, quickly mix everything together for about 10 seconds until the ingredients are just combined and the batter is still a bit lumpy.

Tap the bowl on to the work surface to stop the raising agents working too quickly – you will see the bubbles pop. Spoon the batter evenly into each of the muffin cases and tap the tray on the work surface to pop the bubbles again.

Place in the preheated oven and bake for about 15 minutes. Remove from the oven and place the tray on a wire rack to cool for 10 minutes then transfer the cupcakes in their cases to the wire rack to cool completely.

Once the cupcakes are cool, decorate with Vanilla Buttercream Icing and add your favourite vegan chocolate or sprinkles for extra pizzazz!

BASIC *Chocolate* CUPCAKE

Use the same ingredients as for the Vanilla Cupcakes but use 170 grams (1 ⅓ cups) of self-raising flour mixed with 30g (¼ cup) of cocoa powder. Follow the same method for baking and decorating.

Mint CHOCOLATE CHIP CUPCAKES

It wasn't me who came up with this flavour at Ms. Cupcake. I originally invented a minty one that was much heavier on the chocolate than this light and fluffy beauty. It was a few of the cupcake crew who decided to create a flavour that perfectly replicated – both in look and taste – mint-chocolate-chip ice cream. I think it was our Fibi who was the instigator of this concoction. For a really indulgent treat, pop one of these cupcakes, icing and all, into the freezer for 30 minutes. You'll find the icing really does taste like ice cream!

MAKES 12 LARGE CUPCAKES, 24 FAIRY CAKES OR 48 MINI CUPCAKES

200ml (¾ + 1 tbsp) soya milk
20ml (4 tsp) cider vinegar
170g (1 ⅓ cups)
    self-raising flour
30g (¼ cup) cocoa powder

GLUTEN-FREE? Use a gluten-free self-raising flour blend with ½ teaspoon xanthan gum added.

200g (1 cup) caster sugar
¼ tsp salt
¼ tsp bicarbonate of soda
¼ tsp baking powder
80ml (⅓ cup) light rapeseed
    or other flavourless oil
1 tbsp vanilla extract

½ tsp mint extract, oil,
    or flavouring

FINISHING TOUCHES

a few drops mint extract
    (optional)
½ x quantity Chocolate Spread
    Topping (see page 55)

chocolate, for grating or shaving
1 x quantity Mint Buttercream
    Icing (see page 55)
chocolate chips (optional)

Mix the soya milk and vinegar together. Set aside for 10 minutes. Preheat oven to 180°C/350°F/gas 4. Line your muffin tray with muffin cases.

In a bowl mix the flour, cocoa powder, caster sugar, salt, bicarbonate of soda and baking powder by hand until fully combined. Add the soya milk mixture, the oil, vanilla and the mint extract and, using a metal spoon, quickly mix everything together for about 10 seconds until the ingredients are just combined. Don't mix the batter too much, it should still be a bit lumpy. Tap the bowl on the work surface to stop the raising agents from working too quickly – you will see the bubbles pop. Using an ice-cream scoop or a spoon, place the batter evenly into each of the muffin cases and tap the muffin tray on the work surface to pop the bubbles again.

Place in the oven and bake for about 15 minutes. Cool in the muffin tray on a wire rack for 10 minutes, then transfer the cupcakes in their cases to the rack to cool completely.

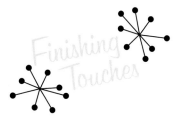

Mix a few drops of mint extract into the Chocolate Spread Topping and slather the mixture thickly on to the cupcakes. Grate or shave some chocolate into the Mint Buttercream Icing and pipe this on top of the chocolate spread layer. Decorate with chocolate chips, if you like, or more chocolate shavings.

RED Velvet CUPCAKES

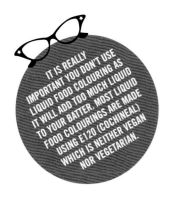

IT IS REALLY IMPORTANT YOU DON'T USE LIQUID FOOD COLOURING AS IT WILL ADD TOO MUCH LIQUID TO YOUR BATTER. MOST LIQUID FOOD COLOURINGS ARE MADE USING E120 (COCHINEAL) WHICH IS NEITHER VEGAN NOR VEGETARIAN.

From the earliest days of the Ms. Cupcake market stall I have had requests for red velvet cupcakes, but I always refused to make them. For those not in the know, a red velvet is more or less just a plain cake dyed to red, and I just couldn't understand what people saw in them. Eventually, I buckled under the pressure, baked my first batch and do you know what? They were pretty great. It's the 'not-too-chocolatey-ness' of the sponge and the 'tang' of the cream cheese icing that seems to work. If you like a red cake, use the food colouring; if not, just leave it out. You will find it's the taste of this cupcake and NOT the appearance that proves its worth.

MAKES 12 LARGE CUPCAKES, 24 FAIRY CAKES OR 48 MINI CUPCAKES

200ml (¾ cup + 1 tbsp) soya milk
20ml (4 tsp) cider vinegar
200g (1¾ cups)
    self-raising flour

200g (1 cup) caster sugar
20g (⅓ cup) cocoa powder
¼ tsp salt
¼ tsp bicarbonate of soda
¼ tsp baking powder

80ml (⅓ cup) light rapeseed
    or other flavourless oil
1 tbsp vanilla extract or essence
½–1 tsp red food colouring paste
    (not liquid)

FOR THE FINISHING TOUCHES

1 x quantity Cream Cheese
    Buttercream Icing
    (see page 54)
red sweets (optional)

GLUTEN-FREE? Use a gluten-free, self-raising flour blend with ¼ teaspoon xanthan gum added.

Preheat oven to 180°C/350°F/gas 4 and line your muffin tray with muffin cases.

Mix the soya milk and vinegar together. Set aside for 10 minutes.

In a large bowl mix the flour, caster sugar, cocoa powder, salt, bicarbonate of soda and baking powder by hand until fully combined. Add the soya milk mixture, the oil, vanilla and the red food colouring paste and, using a metal spoon, quickly mix everything together for about 10 seconds until the ingredients are just combined and the batter is still a little lumpy. Tap the bowl on to the work surface to halt the raising agents from working too quickly – you will see the bubbles pop. Spoon the batter evenly into each of the muffin cases and tap the filled muffin tray on the work surface to pop the bubbles again.

Place in the oven and bake for about 15 minutes. Cool in the tray on a wire rack for 10 minutes, then transfer the cupcakes in their cases to the wire rack to cool completely.

Finishing Touches

Pipe loads of zingy Cream Cheese Buttercream Icing on top and decorate with your favourite red sweet. Alternatively keep one of the cupcake bases aside and crumble it over the rest of the iced cupcakes.

Coconut BOUNTY CUPCAKES

I've always been fascinated by coconuts. When I was a child, back in Canada, I begged my mum to buy me a real one. My father and I puzzled over how to get it open and settled on bashing it repeatedly on the concrete floor of our garage. When that didn't work, we stabbed it with a screwdriver. It finally opened with a whack from our baseball bat. Needless to say we lost all the coconut milk, but that flavour! Whenever I have these cupcakes they transport me back to that cold night in Canada when my love affair with coconuts began.

GLUTEN-FREE? Use a gluten-free self-raising blend flour and add ¼ teaspoon xanthan gum.

MAKES 12 LARGE CUPCAKES, 24 FAIRY CAKES OR 48 MINI CUPCAKES

200ml (¾ cup + 1 tbsp) soya milk
20ml (4 tsp) cider vinegar
170g (1 ⅓ cups) self-raising flour
200g (1 cup) caster sugar
30g (¼ cup) cocoa powder

30g (⅓ cup) desiccated coconut
¼ tsp salt
¼ tsp bicarbonate of soda
¼ tsp baking powder
80ml (⅓ cup) light rapeseed or other flavourless oil
1 tbsp vanilla extract or essence

FOR THE FINISHING TOUCHES

1 x quantity Vanilla Buttercream Icing (see page 54)
a few drops coconut or soya milk
2 big handfuls desiccated or fresh flaked coconut
a few drops coconut extract (optional)
1 x quantity of Chocolate Buttercream Icing (see page 54)

Preheat oven to 180°C/350°F/gas 4. Line your muffin tray with muffin cases. Mix the soya milk and vinegar together. Set aside for 10 minutes.

In a large bowl mix the flour, caster sugar, cocoa powder, coconut, salt, bicarbonate of soda and baking powder together by hand until fully combined. Add the soya milk mixture, the oil and the vanilla and, using a metal spoon, quickly mix everything together for about 10 seconds until the ingredients are just combined. Don't mix the batter too much – it should still be a bit lumpy. Tap the bowl on to the work surface to halt the raising agents from working too quickly – you will see the bubbles pop. Spoon the batter evenly into each of the muffin cases and tap the filled muffin tray on the work surface to pop the bubbles again. Place in the oven and bake for about 15 minutes. Cool the tray on a wire rack for 10 minutes, then transfer the cupcakes in their cases to the wire rack until completely cool.

To make the coconut spread, thin out the Vanilla Buttercream Icing by stirring in a little coconut or soya milk. The texture should be spreadable, not runny. Add a big handful of coconut and the coconut extract if using, and combine.

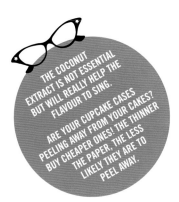

THE COCONUT EXTRACT IS NOT ESSENTIAL BUT WILL REALLY HELP THE FLAVOUR TO SING. ARE YOUR CUPCAKE CASES PEELING AWAY FROM YOUR CAKES? BUY CHEAPER ONES! THE THINNER THE PAPER, THE LESS LIKELY THEY ARE TO PEEL AWAY.

Finishing Touches

Lightly toast another handful of coconut in a non-stick frying pan on a low heat, stirring constantly, and cool to room temperature. Smear a thick layer of the coconut spread on top of each of the cupcakes – be liberal! Alternatively, hollow out a bit of each cooled cupcake with a teaspoon and fill it with the coconut spread. Top the spread with the Chocolate Buttercream Icing and decorate with the lightly toasted coconut.

Bakewell TART CUPCAKES

READ THE BACK OF YOUR GLACÉ CHERRY POT! IF IT CONTAINS THE COLOURING 'CARMINE', 'CRIMSON LAKE', 'COCHINEAL' OR 'E120' THEN IT'S NOT VEGAN.

The Bakewell tart means something different to just about everyone. Maybe you are a fan of the traditional custard dessert set in a flaky pastry which originated in the town of Bakewell, Derbyshire many moons ago. Perhaps it's the fondant and glacé cherry-topped tart that sets your wheels spinning. However you like your Bakewell, you're gonna love this sweet mixture of almond sponge with a big dollop of raspberry jam hidden under the rich almond buttercream.

MAKES 12 LARGE CUPCAKES, 24 FAIRY CAKES OR 48 MINI CUPCAKES

200ml (¾ cup + 1 tbsp) soya milk
20ml (4 tsp) cider vinegar
180g (1⅓ cups) self-raising flour

GLUTEN-FREE? Use a gluten-free, self-raising blend flour with ¼ teaspoon xanthan gum added.

20g (4 tsp) ground almonds
200g (1 cup) caster sugar
¼ tsp salt
¼ tsp bicarbonate of soda
¼ tsp baking powder
80ml (⅓ cup) light rapeseed or other flavourless oil
1 tbsp vanilla extract
1 tsp almond extract

FOR THE FINISHING TOUCHES
a few drops of almond extract

1 x portion Vanilla Buttercream Icing (see page 54)
flaked almonds
raspberry jam
fresh or glacé cherries

Preheat oven to 180°C/350°F/gas 4. Line your muffin tray with muffin cases. Mix the soya milk and vinegar together. Set aside for 10 minutes.

In a large bowl, mix the flour, almonds, sugar, salt, bicarbonate of soda and baking powder together by hand until fully combined. Add the soya milk mixture, the oil, vanilla and almond extracts and, using a metal spoon, quickly mix everything together for about 10 seconds until the ingredients are just combined and the batter is still a little lumpy.

Tap the bowl on to the work surface to stop the raising agents working too quickly – you will see the bubbles pop. Spoon the batter evenly into each of the muffin cases and tap the filled tray on the work surface to pop the bubbles again.

Place in the oven and bake for about 15 minutes. Remove from the oven and cool the muffin tray on a wire rack for 10 minutes before transferring the cupcakes in their cases to the wire rack to cool completely.

Finishing Touches

Add a few drops of almond extract to the Vanilla Buttercream Icing and mix to combine. Put the flaked almonds in a non-stick frying pan and toast on a medium heat, stirring constantly. Remove from the pan to cool.

Spread a big dollop of jam on each cupcake and then pipe your almond buttercream icing over the top to hide the jam below. Decorate with the toasted almond flakes and top it all off with either a fresh or a glacé cherry.

CHOCOLATE *Peanut* BUTTER CUPCAKES

IF YOU DON'T WANT DENSE, FLAT CAKES, THEN BE CAREFUL NOT TO MIX YOUR BATTER TOO MUCH. IT'S FINE TO HAVE LUMPS AND BUMPS AS THEY'LL WORK THEMSELVES OUT IN THE OVEN.

Some flavours are meant to be together and nothing sets off rich chocolate better than the savoury stickiness of peanut butter. I prefer a sweeter, American-style peanut butter, but unsweetened wholenut or seed butters are also fine if that's your thing. Whatever you use, just make sure to decorate the cupcakes with really salty peanuts – the saltiness cuts through the icing and creates a completely crazy party in your mouth.

MAKES 12 LARGE CUPCAKES, 24 FAIRY CAKES OR 48 MINI CUPCAKES

200ml (¾ cup + 1 tbsp) soya milk
20ml (4 tsp) cider vinegar
170g (1⅓ cups) self-raising flour
200g (1 cup) caster sugar

30g (¼ cup) cocoa powder
¼ tsp salt
¼ tsp bicarbonate of soda
¼ tsp baking powder
50g (⅕ cup) peanut butter
80ml (⅓ cup) light rapeseed or other flavourless oil

1 tbsp vanilla extract or essence

FOR THE FINISHING TOUCHES

peanut butter
1 x portion Chocolate Buttercream Icing (see page 54)

1 x portion Peanut Butter Buttercream Icing (see page 54)
salted peanuts, to decorate

GLUTEN-FREE? Use a gluten-free self-raising blend flour with ¼ teaspoon xanthan gum added.

Preheat oven to 180°C/350°F/gas 4. Line your muffin tray with muffin cases. Mix the soya milk and vinegar. Set aside for 10 minutes.

In a large bowl mix the flour, sugar, cocoa powder, salt, bicarbonate of soda and baking powder by hand until fully combined. Add the soya milk mixture, the peanut butter, oil and vanilla and, using a metal spoon, quickly mix everything together for about 10 seconds until the ingredients are just combined. Don't mix the batter too much, it should still be a bit lumpy Tap the bowl on the work surface to stop the raising agents from working too quickly – you will see the bubbles pop. Spoon the batter evenly into the muffin cases and tap the filled muffin tray on the work surface to pop the bubbles again.

Place in the oven and bake for about 15 minutes. Cool in the muffin tray on a wire rack for 10 minutes and then transfer the cupcakes in their cases to the wrack until completely cool.

Finishing Touches

With a knife, spread a thick layer of peanut butter on each of your cupcakes. Alternatively, hollow out a portion from the top of each cake with a teaspoon and carefully fill the hole with the peanut butter.

Fill your piping bag down one side with Chocolate Buttercream Icing and down the other side with Peanut Butter Buttercream Icing. When you pipe this 'split' bag of icing on to your cupcakes you will get a gorgeous swirl effect. Decorate with the saltiest peanuts you can find.

Golden SYRUP CUPCAKES

WHEN BUYING DECORATIONS, LOOK OUT FOR INGREDIENTS LIKE GELATINE, SHELLAC OR BEESWAX AS THESE AREN'T VEGAN.

Vanilla cupcakes are sometimes considered a bit run of the mill. This variation on the basic recipe produces extraordinary results. The flavour and texture will remind you of school dinners and that yummy golden-syrup pudding that always left you looking for seconds. You can of course replace the golden syrup with that vegan staple – agave nectar – and I certainly won't hate you if you replace the golden syrup for indulgent maple syrup either.
Simple, but gorgeous.

MAKES 12 LARGE CUPCAKES, 24 FAIRY CAKES OR 48 MINI CUPCAKES
200ml (¾ cup + 1 tbsp) soya milk
20ml (4 tsp) cider vinegar

GLUTEN-FREE? Use a gluten-free, self-raising flour blend with ¼ teaspoon xanthan gum added.

200g (1¾ cup) self-raising flour
160g (⅓ cup + 1 tsp) caster sugar
¼ tsp salt
¼ tsp bicarbonate of soda
¼ tsp baking powder

80ml (⅓ cup) light rapeseed or other flavourless oil
100ml (¼ cup) golden syrup
1 tbsp vanilla extract or essence

FOR THE FINISHING TOUCHES
drizzles of golden syrup
1 x quantity Vanilla Buttercream Icing (see page 54)
edible gold balls or glitter

Preheat the oven to 160°C/325°F/gas 3 and line your muffin tray with muffin cases.

Mix the soya milk and vinegar together. Set aside for 10 minutes.

In a large bowl mix the dry ingredients by hand until fully combined. Add the soya milk mixture, the oil, 40ml (3 tbsp + 2tsp) of the golden syrup and the vanilla. Using a metal spoon, quickly mix everything together for about 10 seconds until the ingredients are just combined and the batter is still a bit lumpy. Tap the bowl on to the work surface to stop the raising agents working too quickly – you will see the bubbles pop. Spoon the batter evenly into the muffin cases and tap the filled tray on the work surface to pop the bubbles again.

Place in the oven and bake for 14–17 minutes or until an inserted skewer or toothpick comes out clean. Keep checking on them, as golden syrup burns faster than caster sugar. Transfer the tray to a wire rack and, while still in the tray, spoon 1 teaspoon of the remaining golden syrup on top of each cupcake and allow it to seep into the sponge. If you are making fairy cakes or mini cupcakes, reduce the quantity of golden syrup accordingly. Leave to cool for 10 minutes in the tray and then transfer the cupcakes in their cases to the wire rack to finish cooling.

Finishing Touches

Mix a little bit of golden syrup with the Vanilla Buttercream Icing and pipe on top of your cupcakes. Drizzle with additional golden syrup and top with sparkly vegan decorations.

Lemon CHEESECAKE CUPCAKES

When it comes to dessert, my mum thinks cheesecake is as good as it gets, but I didn't share her cheesecake-love when I was growing up – as a lactose-intolerant kid, eating cheesecake always meant a very upset belly. This recipe has the creaminess she loves, but is made in a way my tummy (and soul) can tolerate!

MAKES 12 LARGE CUPCAKES, 24 FAIRY CAKES OR 48 MINI CUPCAKES

200ml (¾ + 1 tbsp) soya milk
juice and finely grated zest of 1 large lemon (you will need approx. 20ml/4 tsp of juice)
200g (1¾ cups) self-raising flour
200g (1 cups) caster sugar

¼ tsp salt
¼ tsp bicarbonate of soda
¼ tsp baking powder
80ml (⅓ cup) light rapeseed or other flavourless oil
1 tbsp vanilla extract
½ tsp lemon extract, oil, or flavouring (optional)

FOR THE FINISHING TOUCHES
THE CRUMBLE

100g (scant 1 cup) plain or self-raising flour
50g (¼ cup) brown or demerara sugar
50g (3 tbsp + 1 tsp) dairy-free margarine, + extra for greasing

THE ICING

1 x quantity Cream Cheese Buttercream Icing (see page 54)
lemon marmalade
lemon zest or candied lemon peel, to decorate

GLUTEN-FREE? Use a gluten-free self-raising flour + ¼ tsp xanthan gum for your cheesecake and wheat-free flour for your crumble.

SHORT OF TIME? MANY OF THE SHOP-BOUGHT CRUMBLE MIXES ARE VEGAN. PREPARE ACCORDING TO THE PACK INSTRUCTIONS. NEED HELP FINDING NON-DAIRY CREAM CHEESE? SEE OUR LIST OF SUPPLIERS (PAGE 152).

Finishing Touches

Preheat the oven to 180°C/350°F/gas 4 and line your muffin tray with muffin cases.

Mix together the soya milk and lemon juice. Set aside for 10 minutes.

In a large bowl mix the lemon zest, flour, caster sugar, salt, bicarbonate of soda and baking powder together by hand until fully combined. Add the soya milk mixture, the oil, vanilla and lemon extract, if using, and, with a metal spoon, quickly mix everything together for about 10 seconds until the ingredients are just combined. Don't mix the batter too much – it should still be a bit lumpy.

Tap the bowl on to the work surface to stop the raising agents working too quickly – you will see the bubbles pop. Spoon the batter evenly into each of the muffin cases and tap the filled tray on the work surface to pop the bubbles again.

Place in the oven and bake for about 15 minutes. Remove from the oven. Keep the oven at the same temperature for the crumble. Cool the muffin tray on a wire rack for 10 minutes before transfering the cupcakes in their cases to the rack to cool completely.

To make the crumble, mix together the flour, sugar and margarine in a bowl using a spoon or your hands, until you have a lumpy crumble. Spread it out evenly on a greased baking sheet and bake in the oven for 8–10 minutes or until the crumble is nicely browned. Cool in the baking tray on a wire rack.

Once the cupcakes have completely cooled, thickly spread the lemon marmalade on top of each one. Pipe the Cream Cheese Buttercream Icing on top and sprinkle with the crumble. Decorate with some lemon zest or candied lemon peel.

CARROT Maple NUT MUFFINS

NUT FREE? NO PROBLEM! THESE MUFFINS TASTE JUST AS FABULOUS WITHOUT THE NUTS.

When we started selling cupcakes at market stalls around London, we had plenty of early morning starts. We found our muffins were perfect breakfasts for our staff while setting up. This flavour was a special favourite of one of our crew, Tracy, for three reasons: she has a mass of ginger hair, which earned her the nickname 'Carrots', she's Canadian, so has to love everything with maple in it, and she's completely nuts.

MAKES 12 VERY LARGE OR 20 MEDIUM MUFFINS

560g (4½ cups) self-raising flour
1 tsp bicarbonate of soda
1 tsp baking powder
120g (2/3 cup) dark brown sugar
2 tsp ground cinnamon
80g (2/3 cup) pecan or walnut pieces, plus extra to decorate
1 large carrot, grated
350ml (1½ cups) soya or rice milk
320ml (1 1/3 cups) light rapeseed or other flavourless oil
100ml (1/3 cup + 1 tsp) maple syrup
2 tsp vanilla extract or essence

FOR THE MAPLE CINNAMON GLAZE

120g (1 cup + 1 tbsp) icing sugar
2 tbsp soya or rice milk
2 tbsp maple syrup
¼ tsp ground cinnamon

Preheat the oven to 180°C/350°F/gas 4 and line your muffin trays with muffin cases.

In a large bowl, mix together the flour, bicarbonate of soda, baking powder, brown sugar, cinnamon and the nuts. Add the grated carrot, soya milk, oil, maple syrup and vanilla. Using a metal spoon, quickly mix everything together for about 10 seconds until the ingredients are just combined. Don't stir the batter too much – it should still be a bit lumpy. Spoon the batter evenly into each of your muffin cases.

Bake in the preheated oven for 20–25 minutes. Cool on a wire rack in the muffin trays for 10 minutes.

While the muffins are cooling, make the glaze by mixing all four ingredients together in a bowl. If it is too firm for your liking, add a couple more drops of milk; if too runny, add a little more icing sugar.

Spoon a tablespoon of the Maple Cinnamon Glaze on to each warm muffin and then transfer the muffins in their cases to the wire rack and allow to cool completely.

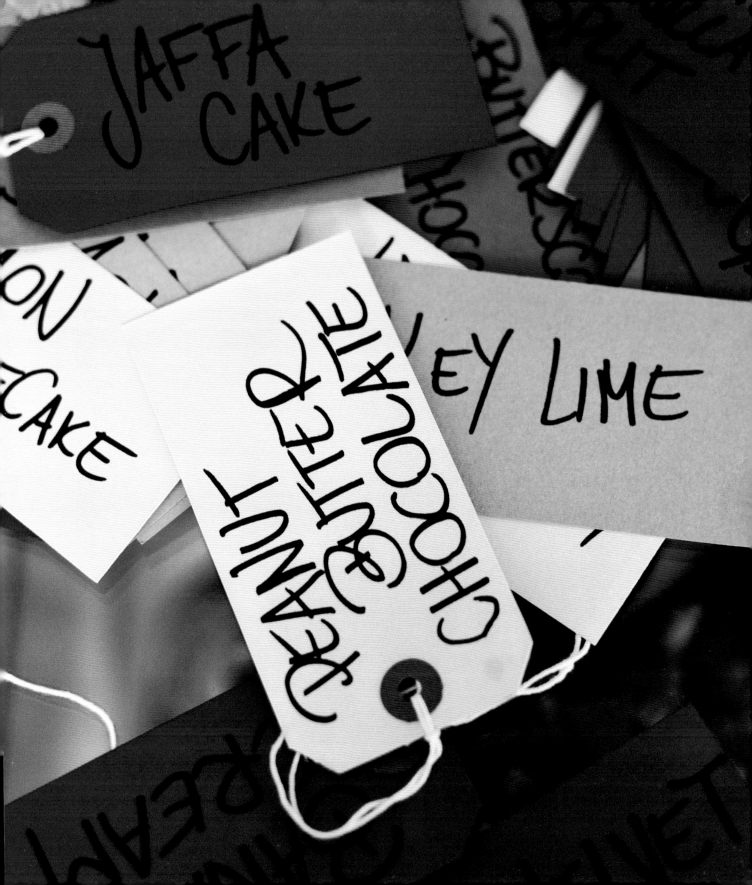

BLUEBERRY *Almond* CRUMBLE MUFFINS

I'm very picky when it comes to blueberry muffins. I hate it when the blueberries bleed into the muffin – there's something so unsettling about a blueish-purpley sponge! The easiest way around this is to drop the blueberries into the batter after spooning it into the muffin trays. This has the added bonus of distributing the berries evenly among the muffins – so no complaints from anyone when you share these around! Now if you want blue tie-dyed muffins, by all means mix those berries in when adding your wet ingredients – they'll taste just as good!

MAKES 12 VERY LARGE OR 20 MEDIUM MUFFINS

FOR THE CRUMBLE

100g (scant 1 cup) plain flour
50g (¼ cup) brown
    or demerara sugar

50g (3 tbsp + 1 tsp)
    dairy-free margarine

FOR THE SPONGE

500g (4 cups) self-raising flour
60g (½ cup) ground almonds
1 tsp bicarbonate of soda

1 tsp baking powder
250g (1¼ cups) caster sugar
500ml (scant 2 cups)
    soya or rice milk
320ml (1⅓ cups) light rapeseed
    or other flavourless oil
2 tsp vanilla extract

½ tsp almond extract or
    flavouring (optional)
100g (about 60) whole blueberries
a handful of flaked
    almonds (optional)

FOR EXTRA AWESOMENESS, REMOVE THE TRAY FROM THE OVEN AFTER 18–20 MINUTES. SPRINKLE FLAKED ALMONDS ON TOP OF THE PARTIALLY COOKED MUFFINS AND RETURN TO THE OVEN TO FINISH BAKING.

YOU CAN USE SELF-RAISING FLOUR FOR THE CRUMBLE IF YOU DON'T HAVE ANY PLAIN FLOUR IN YOUR CUPBOARD.

SHORT OF TIME? MANY OF THE SHOP-BOUGHT CRUMBLE MIXES ARE VEGAN. PREPARE ACCORDING TO THE PACK INSTRUCTIONS.

Preheat oven to 180°C/350°F/gas 4 and line your muffin trays with cases.

To make the crumble, mix the flour, sugar and margarine together in a bowl using a spoon or your hands until you have a lumpy crumble. Set aside.

In a large bowl, mix together the flour, ground almonds, bicarbonate of soda, baking powder and caster sugar. Add the milk, oil, vanilla and almond extracts and, using a metal spoon, quickly mix everything together for about 10 seconds until the ingredients are just combined. Don't mix the batter too much, it should still be a bit lumpy. Spoon the batter evenly into your muffin cases and drop the same amount of blueberries on to each muffin (about 5 for each very large muffin or 3 for each medium-sized one). The blueberries will sink into the batter when baking. Sprinkle each muffin with the crumble.

Bake in the oven for 20–25 minutes. Cool in the muffin trays on a wire rack for 10 minutes, then transfer the muffins in their cases to the rack to cool completely.

STRAWBERRY AND *Banana* MUFFINS

THIS RECIPE WOULD ALSO MAKE A GREAT LOAF CAKE. TRY BAKING THE BATTER IN A LOAF TIN AND INCREASING THE BAKING TIME TO ABOUT 30 MINUTES.

Even us naughty vegans need a bit of wholesome goodness once in a while and I have a particular weakness for a smoothie when I'm feeling low on vitamins. I keep my smoothies simple with a few fruits whizzed together (no wheatgrass for me!). This flavour is an ode to my favourite smoothie combo Strawberry and Banana – a muffin with a wee bit of righteousness thrown in for good measure.

MAKES 12 VERY LARGE MUFFINS OR 20 MEDIUM MUFFINS

560g (4½ cups) self-raising flour
1 tsp bicarbonate of soda
1 tsp baking powder

250g (1¼ cups) caster sugar
1 large over-ripe banana, mashed
350ml (1½ cups) soya or rice milk
320ml (1⅓ cups) light rapeseed or other flavourless oil

2 tsp vanilla extract
12 medium fresh strawberries, hulled and roughly chopped

FOR THE VANILLA GLAZE

120g (1 cup + 1 tbsp) icing sugar
2 tbsp soya or rice milk
½ tsp vanilla extract

Preheat oven to 180°C/350°F/gas 4 and line your muffin trays with cases.

In a large bowl, mix together the flour, bicarbonate of soda, baking powder and caster sugar. Add the mashed banana, the milk, oil, vanilla and chopped strawberries and, using a metal spoon, quickly mix everything together for about 10 seconds until the ingredients are just combined. Don't mix the batter too much, it should still be a bit lumpy. Spoon the mixture evenly into the muffin cases.

Put the muffin tray into the preheated oven and bake for 20–25 minutes. Cool in the muffin tray on a wire rack for 10 minutes.

While the muffins are cooling, make the Vanilla Glaze by mixing together the icing sugar, milk and vanilla in a bowl. If it is too firm for your liking add a couple more drops of milk if too runny, add a little more icing sugar.

Spoon a tablespoon of the Vanilla Glaze on to each warm muffin and then transfer the muffins in their cases to the wire rack to cool completely.

ICINGS and SPREADS

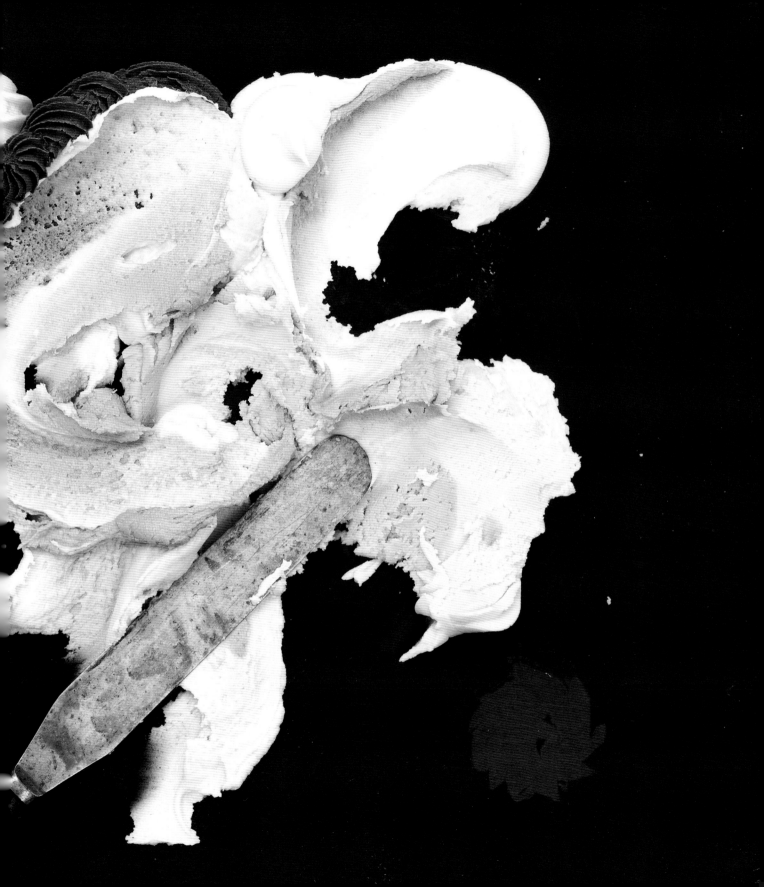

ICINGS *and* SPREADS

We love things sweet at Ms. Cupcake, so the entire shop is generally coated in a thin layer of icing sugar from all the buttercream frosting we make. You may not like things as sweet as we do, so use this sheet as a template for your own experiments. All the recipes make 1 quantity.

Vanilla BUTTERCREAM ICING

75g (5 tbsp) of dairy-free margarine

75g (5 tbsp) of vegetable fat (shortening)

1 tbsp vanilla extract

750g (6 cups) icing sugar

40-60ml (2 tbsp + 2 tsp-¼ cup) soya or rice milk

Using an electric or a hand-held mixer, whip together the margarine, vegetable fat and vanilla until creamy (about 30 seconds). Add half the icing sugar and 40ml (2 tbsp + 2 tsp) milk and continue mixing, slowly at first and then bringing up to speed, until combined. Add the rest of the icing sugar and mix for about a minute until you have a smooth consistency. If the icing is too firm, add a bit more milk and mix; if too soft, add a little more icing sugar.

Chocolate BUTTERCREAM ICING

75g (5 tbsp) dairy-free margarine

75g (5 tbsp) vegetable fat (shortening)

650g (6½ cups) icing sugar

100g (1 cup) cocoa powder

About 80-100ml (⅓ cup-⅓ cup + 4 tsp) soya or rice milk

1 tbsp vanilla extract

Using an electric or a hand-held mixer, whip together the margarine, vegetable fat and the vanilla until creamy (about 30 seconds). Add half of the icing sugar,

all of the cocoa and milk and continue mixing, slowly at first and then bringing up to speed, until combined. Add the rest of the icing sugar and mix for about a minute until you have a smooth consistency. If the icing is too firm, then mix in a bit more milk. If it is too soft, add a bit more icing sugar.

Cream Cheese BUTTERCREAM ICING

25g (1 tbsp + 1 tsp) dairy-free margarine

75g (5 tbsp) vegetable fat (shortening)

125g (⅓ cup + 2 tbsp) soya cream cheese

1 tbsp vanilla extract

about 30-40ml (2 tbsp-2 tbsp + 2 tsp) soya or rice milk

750g (7½ cups) icing sugar

Using an electric or a hand-held mixer, whip together the margarine, vegetable fat, cream cheese and vanilla until creamy (about 30 seconds). Add half of the icing sugar and 30ml (2tbsp) milk and continue mixing, slowly at first and then bringing up to speed, until combined. Add the rest of the icing sugar and mix for about a minute until you have a smooth consistency. If the icing is too firm, then mix in a bit more milk. If it is too soft, add a bit more icing sugar.

Peanut Butter BUTTERCREAM ICING

75g (5 tbsp) smooth peanut butter

75g (5 tbsp) vegetable fat (shortening)

1 tbsp vanilla extract

750g (6 cups) icing sugar

About 80-100ml (⅓ cup- ⅓ cup + 4 tsp) soya or rice milk

Using an electric or a hand-held mixer, whip together the peanut butter, vegetable fat and the vanilla until creamy (about 30 seconds). Add half of the icing sugar and 80ml (¼ cup) milk and continue mixing, slowly at first and then bringing up to speed, until combined. Add the rest of the icing sugar and mix for about a minute until you have a smooth consistency. If the icing is too firm, then mix in a bit more milk. If it is too soft, add a bit more icing sugar.

Mint BUTTERCREAM ICING

75g (5 tbsp) dairy-free margarine	40–60ml (2 tbsp + 2 tsp–¼ cup) soya or rice milk
75g (5 tbsp) vegetable fat (shortening)	½–1 tsp mint extract, oil, or flavouring
1 tbsp vanilla extract	¼ tsp green food colouring paste (not liquid)
750g (6 cups) icing sugar	

Using an electric or a hand-held mixer, whip together the margarine, vegetable fat and the vanilla until creamy (about 30 seconds). Add half of the icing sugar, 40ml (2tbsp) milk, mint extract and colouring paste and continue mixing, slowly at first and then bringing up to speed, until combined. Add the rest of the icing sugar and mix for about a minute until you have a smooth consistency. If the icing is too firm, then mix in a bit more milk. If it is too soft, add a bit more icing sugar.

Custard BUTTERCREAM ICING

75g (5 tbsp) dairy-free margarine	750g (6 cups) icing sugar
75g (5 tbsp) vegetable fat (shortening)	2 tbsp dairy-free custard powder
1 tbsp vanilla extract	40–60ml (2 tbsp + 2 tsp–4 tbsp) soya or rice milk

Using an electric or a hand-held mixer, whip together the margarine, vegetable fat and the vanilla until creamy (about 30 seconds). Add half of the icing sugar, the custard powder, 40ml (2 tbsp + 2 tsp) milk

and continue mixing, slowly at first and then bringing up to speed, until combined. Add the rest of the icing sugar and mix for about a minute until it is a smooth consistency. If the icing is too firm, mix in a bit more milk. If it is too soft, add a bit more icing sugar.

Strawberry BUTTERCREAM ICING

75g (5 tbsp) dairy-free margarine	soya or rice milk
75g (5 tbsp) vegetable fat (shortening)	4–5 strawberries, hulled and finely chopped or 1 tsp strawberry essence
1 tbsp vanilla extract	¼ tsp pink or red food colouring paste (not liquid)
750g (6 cups) icing sugar	
10–30ml (2 tsp–2 tbsp)	

Using an electric or a hand-held mixer, whip together the margarine, vegetable fat and vanilla until creamy (about 30 seconds). Add half of the icing sugar, 10ml (2 tsp) milk, the strawberries (or essence) and colouring paste and continue mixing, slowly at first and then bringing up to speed, until combined. Add the rest of the icing sugar and mix for about a minute until you have a smooth consistency. If the icing is too firm, mix in a bit more milk and mix. If it is too soft, add a bit more icing sugar.

Chocolate SPREAD TOPPING

100g (1 cup) cocoa powder	rapeseed or other flavourless oil
135ml (½ cup + 1 tbsp) light	150ml (⅓ cup) agave syrup

In a bowl, stir all the ingredients until completely combined. If it feels a bit too thick for your liking, add a little extra oil. Once it is thoroughly mixed, pop it into the fridge for about an hour to firm up. It will keep covered in the fridge for up to a week. It's also great in sandwiches!

CAKES and LOAVES

Cakes are often the centrepieces of special occasions – birthdays, weddings, anniversaries – the list goes on. But why do you need to wait for a special occasion to indulge in a slice of moist, handmade cake? Do like I do and find something special to celebrate almost every single day!

Cake is meant to be shared and I've always believed that a sure-fire way to put a smile on someone's face is to offer up a slice. The greatest part of these recipes is that they are suitable for so many different dietary restrictions, so that when you present your creation, no one need miss out on a sweet treat! All the recipes make one cake.

yum!

Victoria SPONGE CAKE

DON'T LEAVE THE LAYERS LINGERING IN THE BAKING TINS OR THE MIDDLE OF YOUR CAKE IS LIKELY TO SINK.

The Victoria sandwich is probably the most traditional of British cakes. When I first moved to the UK I couldn't see what all the fuss was about – after all it is just a plain sponge cake with a bit of jam and cream in the middle. But after making this version it was love at first bite. It was then that I started to see the possibilities – filled with a sweet buttercream frosting or mounds of fresh fruit, this cake would have had Queen Victoria asking for seconds. The Victoria sandwich is usually laden with eggs and butter, but in this ridiculously simple version we eliminate both, retaining instead a light and airy sponge that proves that simple can still be divine.

400g (3 cups + 2 tbsp)
  self-raising flour
240g (1 cup + 3 tbsp) caster sugar
2 tsp baking powder

400ml (1⅔ cup) soya or rice milk
160ml (⅔ cup) light rapeseed
  or other flavourless oil
2 tbsp vanilla extract

FOR THE FINISHING TOUCHES
strawberry jam
1 x quantity Vanilla Buttercream
  Icing (see page 54)

icing sugar or
  fresh strawberries

GLUTEN-FREE? Use a gluten-free self-raising blend flour.

Grease two round 20cm, 23cm or 25cm (8", 9" or 10") cake tins and preheat oven to 180°C/350°F/gas 4.

In a large bowl, mix the flour, sugar and baking powder together. Add the soya milk, oil and vanilla, stirring with a metal spoon until just combined. Tap the bowl on to the work surface to stop the raising agents working too quickly – you will see the bubbles pop. Spoon half of the cake mixture into each of the cake tins and tap the tins on the work surface to pop the bubbles again.

Bake for about 18–20 minutes or until a toothpick, inserted into the middle of the cake, comes out clean. Cool for 10–15 minutes in the tins and then transfer to wire racks to cool completely.

Finishing Touches

To decorate in the traditional fashion, spread the bottom layer with loads of strawberry jam and Vanilla Buttercream Icing and sandwich with the second layer. Dust the top with icing sugar.

Alternatively, do it the Ms. Cupcake way. In addition to the buttercream between the two layers, spread lashings more over the top of the cake and finish with the fresh strawberries.

TURKISH *Delight* CAKE

TRY LOCAL ETHNIC FOOD STORES FOR ROSEWATER AND DRIED ROSE PETALS.

We don't really have Turkish Delight in North America, so please forgive my original belief that Turkish Delight was a gelatine-filled perfumed jelly enrobed in chocolate. When I was given the real thing one Christmas, I swooned with delight. The traditional recipe does not contain gelatine, nor does it come coated in chocolate. The lack of gelatine was something I celebrated, but as I love a chocolate coating on pretty much anything, I came up with this recipe to satisfy. Now, if you don't like rosewater (it is a very strong flavour), leave it out – you'll still be left with an awesome chocolate cake.

340g (scant 2¾ cups) self-raising flour
60g (½ cup) cocoa powder
240g (1 cup + 3 tbsp) caster sugar
2 tsp baking powder
400ml (1 ⅔ cup) soya or rice milk

160ml (⅔ cup) light rapeseed or other flavourless qil
2 tbsp vanilla extract
2 tbsp rose water or 1 tsp rose extract

FOR THE FINISHING TOUCHES

1 x quantity Chocolate or Vanilla Buttercream Icing (see page 54)
a few drops rose extract

¼ tsp red or pink food colouring paste (not liquid)
rose-flavoured Turkish delight and/or dried edible rose petals

GLUTEN-FREE? Use a gluten-free self-raising blend flour.

Grease two round 20cm, 23cm or 25cm (8", 9" or 10") cake tins and preheat oven to about 180°C/350°F/gas 4.

In a large bowl, stir the flour, cocoa powder, caster sugar and baking powder together. Add the milk, oil, vanilla and rose water, stirring by hand until just combined. It is important not to mix the batter too much or your cake won't rise properly. Tap the bowl on to the work surface to stop the raising agents working too quickly – you will see the bubbles pop. Spoon half of the cake mixture into each of the cake tins and tap the tins on the work surface to pop the bubbles again. Bake for about 18–20 minutes or until a toothpick inserted into the middle of the cake comes out clean. Cool for about 10–15 minutes in the tins and then transfer the cakes to wire racks to cool completely.

To make chocolate-rose buttercream, just add a few drops of rose extract to the Chocolate Buttercream Icing. Rose extracts have a very strong flavour, so be careful to not add too much. To make vanilla rose, just add a few drops of rose extract to the Vanilla Buttercream Icing and a tiny amount of red or pink food colouring paste. Both will taste brilliant – you just need to decide if you want a pink iced cake or a super-chocolatey one!

Finishing Touches

Take the bottom layer of your cake and spread with half of your chosen buttercream. Place the second layer on top. Cover the sides of the cake with more buttercream if you like and smear loads on top. Decorate with Turkish delight pieces and/or dried edible rose petals for a truly spectacular presentation.

Rhubarb AND CUSTARD CAKE

I have to admit that I am including this recipe under extreme duress. I may be the only living person in the UK who can't stand rhubarb. However, my team have insisted that I pass on this classy cake recipe to y'all. This cake looks fab and I'm told it tastes damn good – if you like rhubarb.

GLUTEN-FREE? Use gluten-free self-raising blend flour for your cheesecake and wheat-free flour for your crumble.

FOR THE CRUMBLE

100g (scant 1 cup) plain flour
50g (¼ cup) brown or demerara sugar
50g (3 tbsp + 1 tsp) dairy-free margarine

FOR THE SPONGE

400g (3 cups + 2 tbsp) self-raising flour
240g (1 cup + 3 tbsp) caster sugar
2 tsp baking powder
360ml (1½ cups) soya or rice milk
160ml (2/3 cup) light rapeseed or another flavourless oil
100g (½ cup) tinned cooked rhubarb, drained and chopped
2 tbsp vanilla extract or essence

FOR THE FINISHING TOUCHES

1 x quantity Custard Buttercream Icing (see page 55)
30g (1/8 cup) tinned cooked rhubarb
rhubarb and custard sweets

First make the crumble. Preheat the oven to 180°C/350°F/gas 4 and grease a baking sheet. In a bowl, mix together the flour, sugar and margarine using a spoon or your hands until you have a lumpy crumble. Spread it out evenly on the baking sheet and bake in the oven for 8–10 minutes or until the crumble is nicely browned. Remove from the oven and cool in the baking tray on a wire rack.

Grease two round 20cm, 23cm or 25cm (8", 9" or 10") cake tins.

In a large bowl, mix together the flour, sugar and baking powder for the sponge. Add in the soya milk, the oil, the rhubarb and the vanilla, stirring by hand until just combined. It is important not to mix the batter too much or your cake won't rise properly

Tap the bowl on to the work surface to stop the raising agents working too quickly – you will see the bubbles pop. Spoon half of the cake mixture into each of the cake tins and tap the tins on the work surface to pop the bubbles again. Bake for about 18–20 minutes or until a toothpick inserted into the middle of the cake comes out clean. Cool in the tins for about 10–15 minutes then transfer the cakes to a wire rack and cool completely.

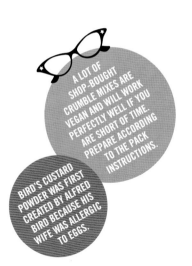

A LOT OF SHOP-BOUGHT CRUMBLE MIXES ARE VEGAN AND WILL WORK PERFECTLY WELL IF YOU ARE SHORT OF TIME. PREPARE ACCORDING TO THE PACK INSTRUCTIONS.

BIRD'S CUSTARD POWDER WAS FIRST CREATED BY ALFRED BIRD BECAUSE HIS WIFE WAS ALLERGIC TO EGGS.

Finishing Touches

Take the bottom layer of your cake and spread liberally with some of the Custard Buttercream Icing. Place the second layer of cake on top. Decorate the sides of the cake with more of the buttercream and coat the iced sides in the crumble, saving some for the top, if you like. Smear the remaining buttercream on top of the cake and work the rhubarb into the remaining icing as you spread it out – this will add flavour and a lovely colour. Decorate with traditional rhubarb and custard sweets or sprinkle with some more crumble.

Neapolitan TRIPLE LAYER CAKE

For a greedy guts like me, who can never choose between desserts, Neapolitan ice cream is the greatest invention this side of Italy. Gosh I love a Neapolitan dairy-free delight! You'll be happy to know that the flavours come through spectacularly in this cake. It really has the wow factor and makes a brilliant birthday cake, regardless of how many candles are on top.

GLUTEN-FREE? Use a gluten-free self-raising blend flour.

FOR THE VANILLA LAYER

200g (1¾ cups) self-raising flour
120g (½ cup) caster sugar
1 tsp baking powder
200ml (¾ cup + 1 tbsp) soya or rice milk
80ml (⅓ cup) rapeseed or other flavourless oil
1 tbsp vanilla extract or essence

FOR THE CHOCOLATE LAYER

170g (1⅓ cups) self-raising flour
2 tbsp cocoa powder
120g (½ cup) caster sugar
1 tsp baking powder
200ml (1 cup) soya or rice milk
80ml (⅓ cup) rapeseed or other flavourless oil
1 tbsp vanilla extract or essence

FOR THE STRAWBERRY LAYER

200g (1¾ cups) self-raising flour
120g (½ cup) caster sugar
1 tsp baking powder
200ml (¾ cup + 1 tbsp) soya or rice milk
80ml (⅓ cup) rapeseed or other flavourless oil
1 tbsp vanilla extract or essence

120g (½ cup) finely chopped fresh strawberries
¼–½ tsp red paste food colouring

FOR THE FINISHING TOUCHES

½–1 x quantity each Chocolate, Vanilla and Strawberry Buttercream (see pages 54-55)
pieces of chocolate strawberries and/or sprinkles

Grease three round 20cm, 23cm or 25cm (8", 9" or 10") cake tins and preheat oven to 180°C/350°F/gas 4.

First, make up the vanilla layer. In a large bow, mix together the dry ingredients – the flour, sugar, and baking powder then in add the wet ingredients – the milk, oil and vanilla to the bowl. Stir by hand until just combined. Do not mix the batter too much – it should still be lumpy – or the cake won't rise properly. Tap the bowl on to the work surface to stop the raising agents working too quickly – you will see the bubbles pop. Spoon the batter into the prepared cake tin and tap the tin on the work surface to pop the bubbles again. Repeat this method for the other two layers – starting by mixing the dry ingredients then adding the wet and just combining before spooning the batter into the prepared cake tins. don't forget to tap each time.

Bake each layer for 18–22 minutes or until a toothpick inserted into the middle of each cake layer comes out clean. Some of the layers may take longer than others, depending on which shelf they are on. Do the skewer test and keep the slower-baking layer in the oven for a bit longer if necessary. Remove from the oven and cool for 10–15 minutes in the tins before transferring the cakes to wire racks to cool completely.

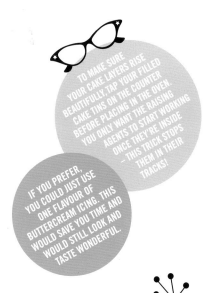

TO MAKE SURE YOUR CAKE LAYERS RISE BEAUTIFULLY TAP YOUR FILLED CAKE TINS ON THE COUNTER BEFORE PLACING IN THE OVEN. YOU ONLY WANT THE RAISING AGENTS TO START WORKING ONCE THEY'RE INSIDE – THIS TRICK STOPS THEM IN THEIR TRACKS!

IF YOU PREFER, YOU COULD JUST USE ONE FLAVOUR OF BUTTERCREAM ICING. THIS WOULD SAVE YOU TIME AND WOULD STILL LOOK AND TASTE WONDERFUL.

Finishing Touches

Spread the chocolate layer with one of the icings (or a mix of all three). Place the vanilla cake layer on to the bottom layer and slather on more buttercream. Finally place the strawberry layer on the top and decorate with all three flavours of buttercream, the chocolate, strawberries, and the sprinkles, if you like.

Blueberry LEMON LOAF CAKE

When I first moved to the UK back in the 90's it was near on impossible to get a fresh punnet of blueberries in my local supermarket. Thankfully nowadays blueberries are plentiful in the UK – but often being shipped in from all over the world. Not to fret! You can still keep things seasonal by changing the berries up in this recipe to raspberries, strawberries, blackberries and so on. Also, don't forget that frozen and tinned berries will do in a pinch as well.

FOR THE SPONGE

250g (2 cups) self-raising flour
150g (¾ cup) caster sugar
½ tsp baking powder
½ tsp bicarbonate of soda

220ml (¾ cup + 2 tbsp)
   soya or rice milk
120ml (½ cup) light rapeseed
   or other flavourless oil

grated zest and juice of 1 lemon
1 tsp vanilla extract or essence
80–100g (1 cup) fresh
   blueberries, with a few
   reserved for decorating

FOR THE LEMON GLAZE

120g (1 cup + 1 tbsp) icing sugar
1 tbsp soya or rice milk
2 tbsp lemon juice,
   grated zest of ½ lemon

MAKE SURE YOU GRATE THE LEMON BEFORE YOU JUICE IT. IT'S RIDICULOUSLY AWKWARD TO TRY AND DO IT THE OTHER WAY AROUND. WE KNOW, WE'VE TRIED!

Grease a 900g (2lb) loaf tin, or line with parchment paper, and preheat oven to 180°C/350°F/gas 4.

In a large bowl, stir the flour, sugar, baking powder and bicarbonate of soda together until thoroughly mixed. Add the soya milk, oil, lemon zest and juice and vanilla and mix together until just combined. Gently fold in the blueberries.

Spoon the batter into the prepared loaf tin and bake for 30–35 minutes or until a toothpick inserted into the middle of the loaf comes out clean. Remove from the oven and cool in the tin for about 10–15 minutes.

Meanwhile, make the Lemon Glaze. Mix together the icing sugar, soya milk, lemon juice and zest in a bowl. If the glaze is too stiff, mix in a couple more drops of milk. If it is a bit too runny, add a bit more icing sugar.

Transfer the cake to a wire rack and cool completely. Once cool, pour over the lemon glaze and decorate with the reserved blueberries if you fancy it.

BANANA-CHOCOLATE *Walnut* LOAF CAKE

This is one of the first things I remember baking as a kid messing about in the kitchen. I suppose that's why it's my 'go-to' cake - the one I bake when I can't think of anything else! Chances are, if you come over to my house for a cuppa this is what I would serve up with it. It's dead simple and has the holy culinary trinity that is banana, chocolate and nut. It also smells fantastic when it's baking so has a real welcoming appeal when someone comes round.

250g (2 cups) self-raising flour
1 tsp baking powder
1 tsp bicarbonate of soda
150g (¾ cup) light brown sugar

250ml (1 cup + 2 tbsp) soya or rice milk
100ml (⅓ cup + 4 tsp) light rapeseed or other flavourless oil

3 over-ripe medium bananas, mashed
2 tsp vanilla extract or essence

50g (¼ cup) dairy-free chocolate chips
80-100g (⅔ - ¾ cup) walnut pieces

I HAVE BEEN KNOWN TO TAKE A COUPLE OF SLICES OF THIS, SPREAD THEM WITH PEANUT BUTTER OR DAIRY-FREE CHOCOLATE SPREAD AND EAT THEM LIKE A SANDWICH. JUST SAYIN'.

IF YOU DON'T HAVE ANY LIGHT BROWN SUGAR IN YOUR CUPBOARD, DARK BROWN SUGAR WILL DO INSTEAD.

Grease a 900g (2lb) loaf tin, or line with parchment paper and preheat oven to 180°C/350°F/gas 4.

In a large bowl, stir the flour, baking powder and bicarbonate together and add in the brown sugar. Mix in the soya milk, oil, bananas and vanilla until just combined, folding in the chocolate chips and walnut pieces at the end.

Spoon the cake mixture into the prepared loaf tin and bake for 30–35 minutes or until a toothpick inserted into the middle of the loaf comes out clean.

Cool for about 10–15 minutes in the tin and then transfer to a wire rack to cool completely. If you can't wait, slice a bit off the end of the cake to eat – it does taste incredible when eaten still warm!

Pineapple UPSIDE-DOWN MINI CAKES

This recipe is a real piece of nostalgia for me. As a kid growing up in the 1970s and '80s the pineapple upside-down cake would take pride of place at any street party, barbeque or family celebration. It may have seriously fallen out of favour, but I say it's time for a revival! Sure you can use fresh pineapple, just sauté the rings in a pan with some margarine first to help soften them. However, if you wanna go 'old skool' with me, it's very likely you have all of the ingredients in your cupboard right now! We split the cake into individual mini cake portions, but if you prefer to bake it in a big cake tin, it will work that way too.

MAKES 12 LARGE MUFFINS, 15 MEDIUM CUPCAKES OR 1 LARGE CAKE

60g (4 tbsp) vegetable margarine

60g (⅓ cup) dark brown sugar
12 tinned pineapple rings (from a 430g tin)
12 glacé cherries
300g (scant 2½ cups)

self-raising flour
180g (¾ cup + 2 tbsp) caster sugar
1½ tsp baking powder
80ml (⅓ cup) pineapple juice (reserved from the tin)

220ml (¾ cup + 2 tbsp) soya or rice milk
120ml (½ cup) light rapeseed or any other flavourless oil
1 tbsp vanilla extract or essence

GLUTEN-FREE? Use a gluten-free self-raising blend flour.

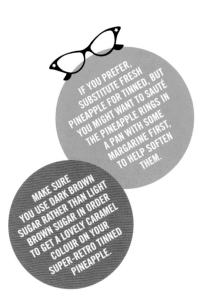

IF YOU PREFER, SUBSTITUTE FRESH PINEAPPLE FOR TINNED, BUT YOU MIGHT WANT TO SAUTÉ THE PINEAPPLE RINGS IN A PAN WITH SOME MARGARINE FIRST, TO HELP SOFTEN THEM.

MAKE SURE YOU USE DARK BROWN SUGAR RATHER THAN LIGHT BROWN SUGAR IN ORDER TO GET A LOVELY CARAMEL COLOUR ON YOUR SUPER-RETRO TINNED PINEAPPLE.

Preheat oven to 180°C/350°F/gas 4. Grease a muffin tray.

In a bowl, mix together the margarine and brown sugar and spread this mixture all over the inside (bottom and sides) of your muffin tray cups. Place one pineapple ring at the base of each cup. If the ring doesn't quite fit in the base, cut a small section away and reshape into a ring. Place a glacé cherry in the hole in the centre of the ring.

In another bowl, mix together the flour, caster sugar and baking powder. Add the pineapple juice, milk, oil and vanilla, mixing until just combined, taking care not to mix the batter too much. The mixture should still have a lumpy texture.

Spoon the cake mixture evenly on top of each pineapple ring until each cup reaches three quarters full. Give the tray a tap on the work surface to stop the raising agents working too quickly and then bake in the oven for about 15 minutes.

Remove from the oven and cool in the tray for about 10–15 minutes before turning out on to a wire rack to cool completely before serving.

EASY-BAKES and NO-BAKES

The traybake is my favourite way of baking. It's simple, easy and hard to mess up! Bars like these make awesome gifts – so bake one batch of each recipe and then slice them all up and create mixed, boxed-up treats for your family, friends and co-workers. That's Christmas sorted!

All of the recipes in this section are made in the same sized tray, so it's up to you how big you want to cut your bars or squares. You can stash most traybakes in the fridge and just cut what you need when you need it, or freeze it in individual portions for tasty treats in the weeks to come.

Here at Ms. Cupcake, we love these recipes most of all. That's because whenever we cut them into slices, we always keep back a slice or two for ourselves without anyone knowing!

Lemon CURD SLICE

TRY MAKING THIS RECIPE WITH LIMES OR ORANGES FOR A CITRUSY SWITCH!

We all love our lemon curd slices here at Ms. Cupcake. Well, almost all of us. Our head baker Sara wishes we would discontinue them completely. Don't get me wrong, she adores their creamy, yet zingy flavour, it's just she is sick to death of zesting lemon rind! Our bakery wouldn't still be open if it wasn't for Sara's commitment and hard graft, but she does whatever she can to avoid grating and juicing those lemons. So if you come to our London shop to try one of these in person and there aren't any left, you know who is to blame!

MAKES 15–24 SLICES

FOR THE SLICE

200g (1½ cups + 1 tbsp) plain flour
80g (scant cup) icing sugar

100g (½ cup) non-dairy margarine
80g (5 tbsp + 1 tsp) vegetable fat (shortening)
grated zest of 1 lemon

FOR THE LEMON CURD

500ml (scant 2 cups) lemon juice (bottled or fresh)
250ml (1 cup + 2 tsp) water
550g (2¾ cups) caster sugar
130g (1 cup + 2 tbsp) cornflour

grated zest of 3 lemons
½ tsp salt
130ml (½ cup + 1 tsp) soya cream
40g (3 tbsp) non-dairy margarine
icing sugar for decoration (optional)

GLUTEN-FREE? Use a gluten-free plain blend flour.

Liberally grease a 33cm x 23cm (13" x 9") cake tin and preheat the oven to 180°C/350°F/gas 4.

In a bowl, mix together the flour, icing sugar, margarine, vegetable fat and lemon zest. Once combined, press the mixture into the prepared tin and bake for about 10 minutes until lightly golden. Remove from the oven and allow the base to cool in the tin for a few minutes.

Meanwhile, make the lemon curd. In a food processor or blender, blend together the lemon juice, water and caster sugar. Pour the mixture into a large pan. Put the cornflour into a separate, small bowl, and add the lemon mixture to the cornflour a few tablespoons at a time, mixing together until you have a smooth thick paste with no lumps. Pour this paste back into the pan and stir to combine. Add the salt and the lemon zest.

On a medium heat, bring the lemon and cornflour mixture to the boil, stirring constantly with a wooden spoon or rubber spatula (about 5 minutes). As the mixture begins to boil you will notice it turns a darker shade of yellow and becomes thick and glossy. Allow the curd to boil for about 1 more minute then remove from the heat. Add the soya cream and the margarine and mix together. Let the mixture sit for 3–4 minutes and then pour the curd evenly on top of the cake in the tin.

Allow to sit at room temperature for at least 30 minutes before placing in the fridge in its tin for at least 2 hours, or until the curd has firmed up to a cut-able consistency.

When you are ready to serve, take the traybake out of the fridge, cut into squares and sprinkle with icing sugar. Store any extra slices covered in the fridge for up to a week.

Nanaimo BARS

CANADIANS DON'T ALWAYS STICK TO THE TRADITIONAL CUSTARD VERSION. DO AS THEY DO AND SWITCH THE CUSTARD POWDER FOR DRIED COFFEE, MINT EXTRACT OR PEANUT BUTTER.

We've heard it pronounced a zillion ways at the shop by many a befuddled British customer demanding, 'What the heck is a Nanaimo bar?' Well, it's a classic Canadian dessert said to have been invented by housewife Mabel Jenkins in Nanaimo, British Columbia, back in the 1950s. At our shop we describe it to the uninitiated as a chocolatey-coconut biscuit base covered in a custard buttercream and topped with a layer of chocolate. We had you hooked when we said 'chocolatey', didn't we? Thought so!

MAKES 15–24 BARS
FOR THE BISCUIT BASE

2 tbsp ground flaxseed
3 tbsp lukewarm water
230g (1 cup) dairy-free margarine
100g (½ cup) caster sugar

90g (scant cup) cocoa powder
250g (2 cups) rich tea or
    digestive biscuits, crushed
200g (3⅓ cups)
    desiccated coconut
100g (¾ cup) chopped
    walnuts (optional)

FOR THE CUSTARD CREAM FILLING

180g (¾ cup) dairy-free margarine
50g (3 tbsp + 1 tsp) vegetable fat
    (shortening)
600g (6 cups) icing sugar
5 tbsp custard powder
2 tbsp soya or rice milk

FOR THE CHOCOLATE LAYER

300g (1½ cups) dairy-free
    chocolate chips or
    chocolate bars
50g (3 tbsp + 1 tsp)
    dairy-free margarine

GLUTEN-FREE? Use vegan gluten-free biscuits.

Liberally grease, or line with parchment paper, a 33cm x 23cm (13" x 9") cake tin.

In a small bowl, whisk the flaxseed with 3 tablespoons of lukewarm water. Set aside for 10 minutes.

Over a low heat, melt the margarine in a pan with the caster sugar and the cocoa powder. Remove from the heat and add the crushed biscuits, coconut, walnuts (if using) and flaxseed mixture. Stir until thoroughly combined. Press the mixture into the prepared cake tin and pop it into the fridge to chill for at least an hour.

Meanwhile, prepare the custard cream filling. Using an electric hand-held mixer, mix together the margarine, vegetable fat, icing sugar, custard powder and soya milk. The custard will resemble a soft buttercream. Take the biscuit layer out of the fridge and spread the custard cream across it evenly.

Finally, for the chocolate layer, melt together the chocolate chips and margarine in a pan over a low heat. Spread the chocolate mixture evenly over the custard cream layer. Return the tray to the fridge. Allow the chocolate to firm up for about an hour before slicing into it. Hum the Canadian national anthem while eating.

CHOCOLATE *Brownies*

Officially, there are two different types of brownie: the fudgy kind and the cake kind. In the UK you only seem to find the fudgy ones, but I have to be honest, they are more difficult to replicate when you cut out the eggs. I have been working on our brownie recipe for two years now and I have tried everything under the sun to replace the eggs, from apple purée, mashed bananas and cooked pumpkin to egg replacement, curdled soya milk and flaxseed, but it was worth it and we are pretty darn pleased with the end result. I present you Ms. Cupcake's brownie recipe – which is a cross between cakey and fudgy to please both our North American and British friends.

MAKES 15–24 BROWNIES
1 tbsp ground flaxseed
3 tbsp of lukewarm water
250g (2 cups) plain flour

60g (½ cup) cocoa powder
300g (1½ cups) caster sugar
100g (½ cup) brown sugar
½ tsp baking powder

½ tsp salt
100ml (⅓ cup + 4 tsp) soya or rice milk
280ml (1 cup + 2 tbsp) rapeseed or other light flavourless oil

1 tbsp vanilla extract or essence
150g (¾ cup) dairy-free chocolate chips or a bar, broken into pieces

GLUTEN-FREE? Use a gluten-free plain blend flour and add ¼ teaspoon xanthan gum.

DID YOU KNOW THAT FLAXSEED AND LINSEED ARE THE SAME THING? WHATEVER IT'S CALLED, TRY TO BUY IT PRE-GROUND TO SAVE YOU THE HASSLE.

IF YOU DON'T HAVE ANY BROWN SUGAR TO HAND, JUST INCREASE THE QUANTITY OF CASTER SUGAR TO 400G (2 CUPS)

Liberally grease, or line with parchment paper, a 33cm x 23cm (13" x 9") cake tin and preheat the oven to 180°C/350°F/gas 4. In a small bowl, whisk the flaxseed with 3 tablespoons of lukewarm water. Set aside for 10 minutes.

In a big bowl, mix together the flour, cocoa, caster sugar, brown sugar, baking powder and salt. Once combined, add in 120ml (½ cup) water, the milk, oil, vanilla, and the flaxseed mixture, stirring together until thoroughly combined. Spoon the mixture into the prepared tin and sprinkle the chocolate chips across the top of the batter. Feel free to add nuts, coconut, dried fruit or whatever else turns your crank!

Bake for about 20 minutes (these Brownies are meant to be gooey, so resist the urge to leave them in the oven for longer). Remove from the oven and cool in the tin on a wire rack. Leave the Brownies in the tin even after you've cut them and wrap the whole tin in clingfilm to retain the moisture.

You can store them, covered, at room temperature for 1 week.

Caramel APPLE NUT BARS

TRY USING FIRM PEARS INSTEAD OF APPLES FOR A TASTY FLAVOUR TWIST.

A couple of years ago, I found a version of this traybake in a magazine, which I cut out and stuffed into my big drawer of 'recipes I need to veganise'. There it sat for a very long time, but every time I opened that drawer somehow it found itself right at the top, as if it was calling, 'Pick Me! Pick Me!' Well, on a cold day in January when we were messing about in the kitchen at Ms. Cupcake, it got its wish and after a few vegan tweaks we found ourselves a winner. I probably don't need to suggest this, but try serving warm with dairy-free ice cream piled on top.

MAKES 15–24 PIECES

FOR THE CARAMEL SAUCE

300g (1½ cups) caster sugar
100g (½ cup) brown sugar
3 tbsp golden syrup

50g (3 tbsp + 1 tsp)
   non-dairy margarine
60ml (¼ cup) soya cream
2 tsp vanilla extract or essence
3 tablespoons plain flour

FOR THE BASE

270g (2 cups + 1 tbsp) plain flour
230g (1¼ cups) brown sugar
180g (1⅔ cup) rolled oats
1 tsp bicarbonate of soda
½ tsp salt

260g (1 cup + 2 tbsp)
   non-dairy margarine
450g (about 3 medium) apples,
   cored, peeled and chopped
70g (heaped ⅓ cup)
   chopped pecans

GLUTEN-FREE? Use a gluten-free self-raising blend flour and gluten-free oats.

Liberally grease, or line with parchment paper, a 33cm x 23cm (13" x 9") cake tin and preheat the oven to 180°C/350°F/gas 4.

First, make the caramel. Put the caster sugar, the brown sugar and golden syrup in a heatproof bowl set over a saucepan of simmering water, on a medium-high heat and melt completely, stirring constantly. Once melted, remove the bowl from the heat and stir in the margarine, soya cream and vanilla. Set aside to cool slightly.

Next, make the base. In a separate bowl, mix the flour, brown sugar, rolled oats, bicarbonate of soda and the salt. Add the margarine, creaming it with a spoon or your hands into the dry mixture. Reserve about 200g (7oz) of this dough to use as the crumble top and press the rest of it evenly into the prepared tin. Bake in the oven for 10–13 minutes.

Just before you take the baked dough out of the oven, add the 3 tablespoons of plain flour to the caramel sauce you made earlier and stir until completely combined.

Remove the tin from the oven and top the baked dough with the chopped apples, pecans and the caramel sauce. Crumble the reserved dough and sprinkle on top.

Return the tin to the oven and bake for a further 20–25 minutes. Remove from the oven and leave in the tin to cool completely on a wire rack. Be patient while the traybake cools – it will be too crumbly to cut while still hot. Trust me, it's worth the wait!

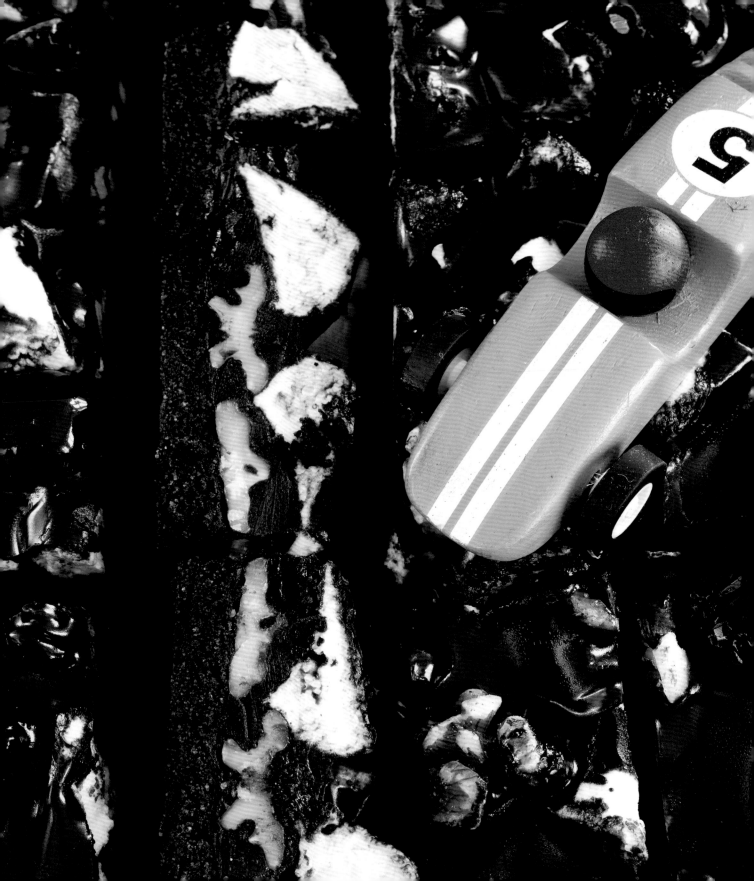

Rocky ROAD BARS

WE USE COARSE GRAIN SEMOLINA – NOT SEMOLINA FLOUR – IN THIS RECIPE BECAUSE IT GIVES AN AMAZING TEXTURE. IF YOU CAN'T FIND COARSE GRAIN SEMOLINA, JUST USE ADDITIONAL PLAIN FLOUR IN ITS PLACE.

If you bring up the subject of 'Rocky Road' at our shop you will probably start a shouting match amongst my Cupcake Crew. My team comes from all over the world, and the recipe for 'Rocky Road' is different in each of their home countries. For North Americans it includes chocolate, marshmallows, walnuts or almonds. For Europeans chocolate and marshmallows feature, but so do biscuits and glacé cherries or even raisins. Although I am the proud holder of both British and Canadian passports, I have to side with the North Americans on this one. Here's the Ms. Cupcake version of Rocky Road — just be aware that if you choose to throw the glacé cherries in, I will be quietly tutting under my breath.

MAKES 15–24 BARS

FOR THE BISCUIT BASE

200g (1 stick +6 tbsp) non-dairy margarine
100g (½ cup) caster sugar

100g (⅔ cup) semolina
170g (1⅓ cups) plain flour
30g (2 tbsp + 1 tsp) cocoa powder

FOR THE TOPPING

500g (2¾ cups) dairy-free chocolate chips or bars broken into pieces
350g (3 sticks) vegetable margarine

30ml (1 tbsp + 1 tsp) golden syrup
150g (1 ⅓ cups) walnuts
20 large vegan marshmallows (or about 40 mini ones)
100g (½ cup) glacé cherries (optional)

GLUTEN-FREE? Replace the flour and semolina with a gluten-free plain flour blend.

Liberally grease, or line with parchment paper a 33cm x 23cm (13" x 9") cake tin and preheat the oven to 180°C/350°F/gas 4.

First, make the biscuit base. In a bowl, cream together with a spoon the margarine and caster sugar. Add in the semolina, flour and cocoa powder and mix together until completely combined. Press this dough evenly into the prepared tin. Bake for about 15–20 minutes. Remove from the oven and cool the tin on a wire rack for about 15 minutes.

Next make the topping. In a pan, melt the chocolate, margarine and golden syrup over a low heat. Remove the pan from the heat and allow to cool for 5 minutes before adding the nuts and half the marshmallows (and glacé cherries if using). Pour the chocolate and nut mixture on top of the biscuit base in the tin and then sprinkle the remaining marshmallows on top. Chill in the fridge for 2 hours until firm before serving. To store, keep the tin covered in the fridge for up to 1 week.

We have Gift Vouchers

Come In
WE'RE
OPEN

Kitchen SINK BARS

The idea behind this tiffin-like fridge cake is that it gives you the opportunity to use up bits of ingredients lurking at the back of your cupboard. It really is impossible to mess up, so think of this as a template to work from rather than a steadfast recipe. Just keep proportions the same, even if you are missing some ingredients. You really can throw anything in, well, everything but the kitchen sink!

MAKES 15–24 BARS

500g (2¾ cups)
   dairy-free chocolate
200g (1 stick + 6 tbsp)
   non-dairy margarine

GLUTEN-FREE Use gluten-free cereals and biscuits.

100ml (1/3 cup + 4 tsp)
   golden syrup
about 25 digestive or rich tea
   biscuits, broken into quarters

100g (¾ cup) nuts, any kind
   (walnuts, pecans or
   peanuts all work well)
75g (2¼ cups) crisped rice cereal

75g (2¼ cups) cereal flakes
   (we use corn flakes)
100g (¾ cup) dried fruit,
   any kind (we like cherries,
   raisins or cranberries)

Liberally grease, or line with parchment paper, a 33cm x 23cm (13" x 9") cake tin.

Melt the chocolate and margarine in a very large pan over a low heat. Add the golden syrup and stir until melted and combined. Remove the pan from the heat and stir in all of the remaining ingredients. Press the mixture evenly into the prepared tin and pop it into the fridge. It should be set within 2 hours.

This recipe is really rich, so cut into small slices. Store this no-bake covered in the fridge and it will keep for up to 1 week.

Raspberry ALMOND CRUMBLE SQUARES

THE VARIATIONS FOR THIS ARE ENDLESS. USE ANY FLAVOUR OF JAM AND FRUITS YOU LIKE. TINNED FRUITS WILL ALSO DO IN A PINCH!

One of the reasons I started Ms. Cupcake was that I couldn't find the decadent, cruelty-free desserts I craved. I was sick of being offered plain flapjacks as the only vegan option when out and about. Not that I'm against flapjacks – in fact, my Welsh husband has a serious flapjack addiction – but if I'm gonna go to the bother of baking my own, I'm certainly gonna add some pizzazz to the recipe! I guess that's what these bars are, flapjacks disguised as something far more glamorous.

MAKES 15–24 SQUARES

350g (2¾ cups) plain flour
300g (3 cups) rolled oats
150g (¾ cup) brown sugar
150g (¾ cup) caster sugar

GLUTEN-FREE Use a gluten-free self-raising blend flour and gluten free oats.

50g (⅓ cup) ground almonds
½ tsp bicarbonate of soda
½ medium banana, mashed
2 tsp vanilla extract
250g (2¼ sticks + 2 tbsp) vegetable margarine

1 tsp almond extract (optional)
350g (1½ cups) raspberry jam
300g (2½ cups) fresh or frozen raspberries (or tinned raspberries, drained)
a handful of flaked almonds

FOR THE CRUMBLE

50g (scant ½ cup) plain flour
50g (scant ½ cup) rolled oats

Liberally grease, or line with parchment paper, a 33cm x 23cm (13" x 9") cake tin and preheat the oven to 180°C/350°F/gas 4.

In a big bowl mix together the flour, oats, brown sugar, caster sugar, ground almonds and bicarbonate of soda. Add the mashed banana, vanilla, margarine and almond extract (if using) and mix together using your hands or a spoon. Set about 350g (12oz) of this dough aside for the crumble topping and then spread the rest of the mixture evenly into the prepared pan. Spread the jam and fruit over the top.

To make the crumble topping, mix the reserved dough with the flour and oats and work together until you have crumbly texture. Sprinkle this crumble on top of the fruit layer.

Bake for about 15 minutes in the oven, sprinkle with flaked almonds and return to the oven for an additional 10 minutes or so. Remove the tin from the oven and set on a wire rack to cool completely. Slice into individual portions in the tin and tuck in! Store in an airtight container at room temperature for up to 1 week.

Snap BARS

MAKE THIS RECIPE IN MUFFIN TINS TO GET PERFECTLY FORMED INDIVIDUAL TREATS.

We spent a long time thinking about what to name these bars. Whenever we invent something new at the bakery I ask my team for suggestions. Jhenn usually comes up with a ludicrous name, loosely based on some obscure pop-culture reference that no one else understands. Needless to say, Jhenn doesn't get to name many things at the bakery. She may not have made up the name for these, but she certainly makes these in a snap. See what I did there? Enjoy this quick and easy 'no-bake' and sprinkle it with a few Jhenn-like bad jokes for good measure.

MAKES 15–24 BARS

350g (1 cup) golden syrup

230g (1 cup + 2 tbsp) caster sugar

425g (1¾ cups) peanut butter (American is best, but any will do)

210g (6 cups) crisped rice cereal

300g (1½ cups) dairy-free chocolate chips

50g (3 tbsp + 1 tsp) dairy-free margarine

GLUTEN-FREE? Use gluten-free cereal.

Liberally grease, or line with parchment paper, a 33cm x 23cm (13" x 9") cake tin.

Melt the golden syrup and caster sugar in a large pan over a medium heat. Add the peanut butter and stir until all melted and combined. Remove the pan from the heat and stir in the crisped rice cereal, making sure it is thoroughly coated in the peanut butter mixture. Press evenly into the prepared tin and set aside.

In a separate heatproof pan, melt the chocolate chips and margarine. Remove from the heat and, using a spatula, spread the chocolate mixture over the crisped rice layer. Allow to set at room temperature or in the fridge if you want it quicker! It should set within the hour. Cut into bars or squares and enjoy.

COOKIES

I love a cookie. Crunchy, chewy, crisp or cakey — any kind will do! Here we have taken American cookies and British biscuits and mashed them up to create some fabulous vegan delights. Need more than the recipe gives you? Just make a double batch. Need less? Make the whole recipe and refrigerate or freeze the dough you don't need straight away. For me, a warm handmade cookie sends me reeling back in time — it kinda feels like getting a kiss from my mamma. So bake some of these up, and when you bite into one, imagine you're getting a big smacker from me!

yum!

Chocolate CHIP COOKIES

FOR DOUBLE-CHOCOLATE CHIP COOKIES, REPLACE 30–40G (2 HEAPED TBSP) OF THE FLOUR WITH COCOA POWDER.

What says 'love' better than a chewy, yet crisp, Chocolate Chip Cookie? We don't use commercially made, egg-replacement powder very much at the bakery because we like to keep our ingredients simple. We have tried making this recipe with fruit purées or flaxseed mixtures, but for these cookies to be this indulgent, the egg replacer works the best. You could try throwing in some nuts or switch 'em up to be filled with raisins or dried cranberries for a more wholesome kick.

MAKES ABOUT 10 BIG OR 18 MEDIUM COOKIES

400g (3 cups + 2 tbsp) plain flour
2 tsp baking powder
1 tsp bicarbonate of soda
150g (¾ cup) dairy-free chocolate chips
150g (1¼ sticks/10 tbsp) non-dairy margarine
75g (5 tbsp) vegetable fat (shortening)
150g (¾ cup) caster sugar
170g (scant 1 cup) brown sugar
1 tbsp vanilla extract or essence
3 tsp egg-replacement powder
3 tbsp lukewarm water

Preheat oven to 180°C/350°F/gas 4 and liberally grease 2 large baking sheets or line them with parchment paper.

In a large bowl, mix together the flour, baking powder and bicarbonate of soda. Stir in the chocolate chips and set aside. In a separate bowl, cream together the margarine, vegetable fat, caster sugar, brown sugar and vanilla. Set aside.

In a third small bowl, whisk together the egg-replacement powder and lukewarm water until light and frothy. Pour this frothy mixture into the bowl with the flour, then add the margarine mixture and combine with your hands or a spoon.

Form the dough into 18 medium balls (or 10 balls for giant cookies) and place on the prepared baking sheets, leaving a couple of inches between them to allow them room to spread as they cook. Bake for 12–13 minutes for medium cookies or 15–16 minutes for the large ones. They should have a golden colour and still be soft to the touch. As soon as you take the sheets out of the oven, whack them on the counter top to flatten the cookies out and give them the desired chewy texture. Cool on the sheets on a wire rack for a couple of minutes before transferring the cookies with a spatula to the wire rack to cool completely.

Peanut BUTTER COOKIES

My love of peanut butter is well known. If I could get away with putting peanut butter in everything we make, I would. Mamma-Cupcake (that's my mum), used to be a fan of the stuff, but she's not such a big fan anymore. I reckon the reason comes from my insistence as a child to ALWAYS have peanut butter and jam sandwiches in my packed lunch. I don't mean mostly – I mean every single day for every single year of primary school. Every time I bake these cookies up, I think of my long-suffering mum and the years of culinary boredom I must have put her through. Thanks Mamma!

MAKES 18 COOKIES

275g (1 cup + 5 tsp) creamy peanut butter (American is best, but any will do)

125g (9 tbsp) dairy-free margarine
140g (½ cup + 1 tsp) maple syrup

85g (⅓ cup + 2 tsp) caster sugar
70g (⅓ cup) brown sugar

1 tbsp vanilla extract or essence
240g (scant 2 cups) plain flour

IF YOU USE NATURAL (NO ADDED SUGAR) PEANUT BUTTER OR A DIFFERENT KIND OF NUT OR SEED BUTTER, THE COOKIES WILL BE DENSER AND WON'T SPREAD AS MUCH – BUT WILL STILL TASTE FAB!

ADD A HANDFUL OF CRUSHED PEANUTS FOR EXTRA CRUNCH.

Preheat oven to 160°C/325°F/gas 3 and liberally grease 2 large baking sheets or line them with parchment paper.

In a large bowl, cream together all of the ingredients, except the flour. Once mixed, slowly add the flour to the mix and stir until combined. Using a spoon, form about 18 balls of dough and place on the prepared baking sheets, leaving a couple of inches between them to allow them room to spread as they cook. Press the balls down with a fork in a criss-cross manner to leave decorative indents and flatten out the dough. You may need to dip your fork into a bit of extra flour if the dough is sticking to it.

Bake for 15 minutes. As you remove the sheets from the oven, whack the tray on your counter to flatten out the cookies. Leave them on the sheets to cool on a wire rack for a couple of minutes, then transfer them to the wire rack using a spatula to cool completely.

Jammy DODGERS

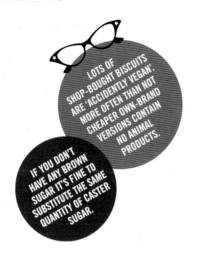

LOTS OF SHOP-BOUGHT BISCUITS ARE 'ACCIDENTLY VEGAN'. MORE OFTEN THAN NOT CHEAPER OWN-BRAND VERSIONS CONTAIN NO ANIMAL PRODUCTS.

IF YOU DON'T HAVE ANY BROWN SUGAR IT'S FINE TO SUBSTITUTE THE SAME QUANTITY OF CASTER SUGAR.

You could call these Linzer biscuits as they are a variation on the German classic, but vegans all over Britain are thankful that Burton's Biscuits, the makers of the official Jammie Dodgers, make them to a vegan recipe. Vegans are known to eat Jammie Dodgers by the packet-load, so this is our homage to the kiddie favourite. If you don't fancy making jam-filled cookies, use the dough on its own to create the world's simplest rolled sugar cookies. The great thing about this recipe is that the dough will keep in the fridge for a good week so you can roll, cut and bake just a few cookies at a time. That way, you won't scoff the whole lot at once!

MAKES 12–36 BISCUITS DEPENDING ON THE SIZE OF YOUR CUTTERS

350g (2¾ cups) plain flour
1 tsp bicarbonate of soda
a pinch of salt
140g (9 tablespoons + 2 tsp) dairy-free margarine
100g (½ cup) brown sugar
3 tbsp golden syrup
1 tbsp vanilla extract
seedless raspberry or strawberry jam (or another flavour if you prefer)
icing sugar, for dusting (optional)

Preheat the oven to 180°C/350°F/gas 4 and grease 2 baking sheets or line with parchment paper.

In a bowl mix together the flour, bicarbonate of soda, and salt. In a separate bowl, cream together the margarine, sugar, golden syrup and vanilla. Slowly add the flour mixture into the margarine mixture, stirring to combine using a spoon or your hands until it comes together as a dough. Wrap the dough in clingfilm and put it in the fridge to chill for a minimum of 30 minutes (although it can stay there for a couple of days if you want to wait before baking.)

Roll out the dough on a lightly floured surface until about a 3mm (1/8 inch) thick. Using a cookie cutter, cut out as many shapes as you can (this is dependent on how big you want the cookies). Using a very small cookie cutter or a very sharp knife, cut out a shape from the middle of half of them (this is where the jam will peek through).

Bake the cookies for 8–12 minutes. You want them cooked through, but not browned. Remove from the oven and cool on the sheets on a wire rack for a couple of minutes before transferring the cookies to the rack with a spatula to cool completely.

Once they have cooled, spread the whole cookies with a dollop of jam. Place the cookies with the peek-a-boo window on top, allowing a little of the jam to peek through. Sprinkle with icing sugar, if you like and serve.

Snickerdoodles (CINNAMON COOKIES)

REMEMBER, THERE ARE NO EGGS IN THESE COOKIE DOUGHS, SO THEY'RE ENTIRELY SAFE TO EAT UNCOOKED!

Okay, so strictly speaking these aren't traditional Snickerdoodles. In case you are wondering, Snickerdoodle is the name those on the other side of the Atlantic have given to sugar cookies that have been rolled in cinnamon-sugar prior to baking. The Ms. Cupcake version is a fusion of our Chocolate Chip Cookie dough (minus the chocolate) and a classic Snickerdoodle. I imagine traditionalists will be shouting angrily when they read this, but who cares? Our non-conformist ways leave you with chewy, gooey, melt-in-your mouth cinnamonny bliss.

MAKES ABOUT 10 BIG OR 18 MEDIUM COOKIES

400g (3 cups + 2 tbsp) plain flour
2 tsp baking powder
1 tsp bicarbonate of soda
4 tbsp ground cinnamon
150g (1¼ sticks/10 tbsp) dairy-free margarine
75g (5 tbsp) vegetable fat (shortening)
250g (1¼ cups) caster sugar
170g (scant 1 cup) brown sugar
1 tbsp vanilla extract or essence
3 tsp egg-replacement powder
3 tbsp lukewarm water

Preheat the oven to 180°C/350°F/gas 4 and liberally grease 2 large baking sheets or line them with parchment paper.

In a large bowl, mix together the flour, baking powder, bicarbonate of soda and 2 tablespoons of the cinnamon. Set aside.

In a separate bowl, cream together the margarine, vegetable fat, 150 grams (¼ cup) of the caster sugar, the brown sugar and vanilla.

In a third bowl, whisk together the egg replacement powder with the lukewarm water until it is light and frothy.

Add the egg mixture and the creamed margarine to the bowl with the flour and combine everything together using either your hands or a spoon.

In a small, separate bowl, mix together the remaining caster sugar and the rest of the cinnamon.

Form the dough into 18 balls (or 10 for giant cookies) and roll each ball in the cinnamon sugar mixture until fully coated. Place the balls on the prepared baking sheets, leaving a few inches between them to allow them room to spread as they cook. Bake for about 12–16 minutes. Remove from the oven and whack the sheets on your counter to flatten out the cookies. Cool on the baking sheet on a wire rack for a couple of minutes, before transferring the cookies to the wire rack using a spatula to cool completely.

Jaffa CAKES

BISCUIT OR CAKE? ACCORDING TO THE TAXMAN IT'S DEFINITELY A CAKE – MEANING YOU DON'T PAY TAX ON JAFFA CAKES. TO BE HONEST, MY BELLY DOESN'T CARE EITHER WAY!

Our customers begged us to veganize Jaffa Cakes right from the beginning, so clearly there is some serious love for the chocolate-orange biscuit-cake. Now, I like my recipes simple and I'm not one for sticking to convention, so please don't burn me at the stake when you see I'm substituting marmalade for the orange jelly. 'Gasp!' I hear. If you want to be a purest, make a batch of vegan orange jelly and cut into discs to place on the top of each cake before coating with chocolate. Just remember, we'll already be eating our non-traditional jaffa cakes while you're still waiting for your jelly to set!

MAKES 12–15 JAFFA CAKES

100g (scant 1 cup) self-raising flour
60g (¼ cup + 1 tbsp) caster sugar

100ml (⅓ cup + 4 tsp) soya or rice milk
50ml (3 tbsp + 1 tsp) light rapeseed or other flavourless oil)
1 tsp vanilla extract or essence

FINISHING TOUCHES

150g (¾ cup) dairy-free chocolate chips, or a bar broken into pieces

50g (3 tbsp + 1 tsp) dairy free margarine
grated zest of ½ orange
12–15 tsp orange marmalade

GLUTEN-FREE? Use gluten-free self-raising blend flour.

Grease a bun tray. Preheat the oven to 180°C/350°F/gas 4.

In a medium bowl, mix together the flour and caster sugar. Add the milk, oil and vanilla, stirring until just combined. Drop a small spoonful of the batter into each of the holes in the prepared tray and bake for about 8 minutes. Remove from the oven and cool in the tray for 2 minutes before turning the bases out on to a wire rack to cool completely.

Melt the chocolate and margarine in a pan on a low heat, stirring constantly until combined. Remove from the heat and add the orange zest.

Once the cakes have cooled, and before removing them from the wire rack, spoon a dollop of orange marmalade on top of each one. Spoon the chocolate evenly over the cakes so that the tops are completely covered. The excess chocolate can drip through the wire rack leaving the bottoms free of chocolate. Refrigerate on the rack for about 20 minutes until set. Keep these bad boys refrigerated until you are ready to serve them.

Cookie SANDWICHES

Cookies are great — there is no denying it. But here at Ms. Cupcake we don't just settle for great — we want the best. So we take not one, but two, of our cookies, sandwich them together with lashings of buttercream and other good things, and voilà — we give you the incredible Cookie Sandwich. There are no rules here. Get creative, but here are a few of our favourites to get you started!

CHOCOLATE CHIP COOKIE SANDWICH

Pipe or spread a layer of **Vanilla or Chocolate Buttercream Icing** (see page 54) on to the flat side of **1 Chocolate Chip Cookie** (see page 102) and sandwich **a second Chocolate Chip Cookie** on top. Press lightly until the buttercream starts to peek out at the sides. Roll the exposed icing in **chocolate chips or sprinkles** for extra bling!

PEANUT BUTTER AND JAM COOKIE SANDWICH

Pipe or spread a layer of **Peanut Butter Buttercream Icing** (see page 54) on to the flat side of **1 Peanut Butter Cookie** (see page 107). Spread the flat side of **a second Peanut Butter Cookie** with a layer of **peanut butter** and top with a layer of **strawberry or other flavour jam**. Sandwich the two cookies together and press lightly until the jam and buttercream start to peek out at the sides.

SNICKERDOODLE COOKIE SANDWICH

Mix a teaspoon or two of ground cinnamon into 1 quantity of **Vanilla Buttercream Icing** (see page 54). Pipe or spread a layer of this **Cinnamon Buttercream Icing** on to the flat side of **1 Snickerdoodle** (see page 113). Sandwich **a second Snickerdoodle** on top and press slightly until the buttercream starts to peek out at the sides.

FOR AN EXTRA SPECIAL TREAT, SWAP THE BUTTERCREAM FOR DAIRY-FREE ICE CREAM. OH BABY!

NAUGHTIEST of THEM ALL

I make no excuses for this chapter. Pretty much everything in it is super-sugary and deep-fried – what we call 'dirty' food here at Ms. Cupcake. These recipes are certainly not for calorie counters, overly health-conscious folk or faint-hearted souls. What you have instead is a collection of ridiculously indulgent treats that you can dip into whenever you are feeling particularly naughty. As long as you don't use this chapter as a weekly diet plan!

We've always set out to turn veganism on its head at Ms. Cupcake, so whip up some of these sticky, crispy and gooey delights to blow the minds of any vegan naysayer. Just don't forget the napkins 'cause you're gonna need them!

Doughnuts AND DOUGHNUT HOLES

MAKE JAM-FILLED TREATS BY NOT CUTTING THE HOLE OUT AND FRYING FOR A FEW EXTRA MINUTES BEFORE INJECTING YOUR FAVOURITE JAM INSIDE.

There must not be a single person on this planet that doesn't swoon at the smell of hot, freshly made doughnuts. My absolute favourite thing to eat is the hole – the dough cut out from the middle that is so often discarded. These little balls of pleasure are sold in their own right in both the US and Canada, so why the Brits haven't cottoned on to them yet, I'll never know! These doughnuts are best eaten on the day they're made, but if you want to keep them a day or two extra, just pop them in the microwave to reheat prior to serving.

MAKES 8 RINGS AND HOLES

40g (3 tbsp) vegetable margarine
170ml (²/₃ cup + 4 tsp) soya or rice milk

½ teaspoon salt
40g (3 tbsp) caster sugar
1 tbsp vanilla extract or essence
340g (scant 2¾ cups)

self-raising flour
7g (2¼ tsp) dried active yeast
1 x quantity Vanilla Glaze (see page 51),

cinnamon sugar, caster sugar or icing sugar
light rapeseed or other flavourless oil, for deep-frying

In a pan, melt the margarine over a low heat. Add the milk, salt, sugar and vanilla, taking care not to boil, then remove from the heat and set aside to cool a little.

In a large bowl, mix the flour with the yeast until combined. Add in the margarine mixture and work with your hands for at least 10 minutes – first bringing the ingredients together and then kneading the dough on a lightly floured surface. Return the kneaded dough to the bowl and cover loosely with cling film or a damp tea towel. Leave to rise in a warm area for 1 hour until the dough has doubled in size.

Roll out the dough to about 2cm (1 inch) thick and cut out 8 circle shapes. Using a smaller cutter or a shot glass, cut a hole in the middle of each doughnut, reserving the dough you cut from the centres – these will be your doughnut holes! Lightly cover everything again and leave in a warm area for another hour to rise for a second time.

To fry your doughnuts, heat the oil in a deep-sided pan or a deep-fat fryer, to about 160°C/325°F, or until a cube of bread dropped into the hot oil turns golden in 15 seconds.

Fry the doughnut holes and rings in small batches until golden brown. Remove from the hot oil with a slotted spoon and transfer them to a wire rack to drain. While still warm, coat the doughnuts in the Vanilla Glaze, roll in the cinnamon sugar or sprinkle with sugar before serving.

Apple FRITTERS

TRY MAKING LOADS OF MINI FRITTERS AND SERVE THEM UP IN A DISH WITH DAIRY-FREE WHIPPED CREAM.

Doughnuts are great, but yeast is a tricky beast, so when we were working on our recipe for Apple Fritters we decided to go for more of a cake concoction and eliminate the need for yeast. They're also much quicker to make – no pesky rising time required – so you can get these in your belly in a much speedier fashion. Apple Fritters might not be the prettiest of sweet treats, but that apple-cinnamon goodness is enough to make anyone weak at the knees with delight.

MAKES 6

140g (1 cup + 1 tbsp) plain flour
60g (¼ cup + 1 tbsp) caster sugar
½ tsp salt

1½ tsp baking powder
1½ tsp ground cinnamon
90ml (⅓ cup + 2 tsp) soya or rice milk

50ml (¼ cup) plain, vanilla or coconut soya yoghurt
1 tsp vanilla extract
2 medium apples, peeled, cored and finely chopped

light rapeseed or other flavourless oil, for deep-frying
1 x quantity Maple Cinnamon Glaze (see page 43)

Heat the oil in a deep-sided pan or a deep fat fryer, to about 180°C/350°F, or until a cube of bread dropped into the hot oil turns golden in 15 seconds.

In a large bowl mix together the flour, sugar, salt, baking powder and cinnamon. Add the milk, yoghurt, vanilla and apple and stir until fully combined. Drop one big spoonful of the batter at a time into the hot oil, frying the fritters in small batches until golden brown (about 4 minutes), turning them as you go.

Remove from the heat and transfer the fritters to a wire rack to drain. While still warm coat them in the Maple Cinnamon Glaze. Leave them on the wire rack for a couple of minutes for the glaze to firm up before serving.

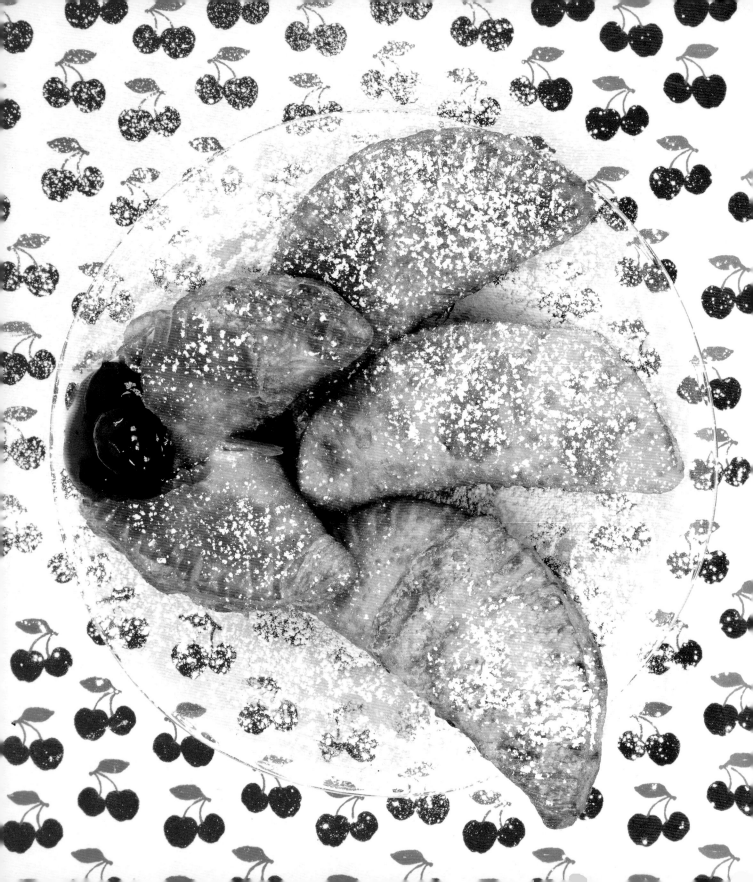

EASY *Fried* PIE

This is by far the easiest recipe in the book. I don't even think it actually is a recipe – you can choose the quantities to suit your taste (or what you have in the fridge) – I'm just letting you know that if you fry these two shop-bought ingredients together, your friends and family will think that you are the most amazing chef on the planet. The other awesome thing about this recipe is that you only need to make one at a time, so if you are the type who eats an entire tray of brownies you just made *ahem* this is the solution to your 'I need something sweet NOW!' craving. Remember, sometimes life's too short to make your own pastry!

MAKES 1 PIE

DON'T LIKE THE IDEA OF FRYING YOUR PIE? YOU CAN POP THESE INTO THE OVEN AT ABOUT 190°C/375°F/GAS 5 FOR 8–10 MINUTES INSTEAD.

MOST SHOP-BOUGHT PASTRY IS VEGAN, BUT AVOID 'BUTTER' PUFF PASTRY.

a block of dairy-free ready-roll puff pastry (any shop-bought brand)

fruit filling, tinned or frozen (apple or cherry work well)

light rapeseed or other flavourless oil, for frying
icing sugar (optional)

Heat about 2cm (1 inch) of oil in a pan to about 180°C/350°F, or until a cube of bread dropped into the hot oil turns golden in 15 seconds.

Cut a 2cm (1 inch) chunk of puff pastry from the pastry block and roll it out until it's about ½cm (¼ inch) thick. Roll into a square to make a triangular pie. If you want to get fancy, cut the pastry into a circle using a cutter or shot glass for a crescent-shaped pie. Put a dollop of pie filling in the middle and fold the pasty over it. Seal the pie by pressing the pastry edges together with the prongs of a fork.

Fry the pie in the hot oil for a minute or so on each side. Blot with kitchen paper and serve warm with a dusting of icing sugar.

Funnel CAKES

IT'S NOT JUST THE NORTH AMERICANS THAT LOVE SPIRAL-SHAPED FRIED DOUGH! IN AUSTRIA AND ITALY THESE ARE KNOWN AS STRAUBEN, IN FINLAND TIPPALEIPÄ, AND A SIMILAR INDIAN TREAT IS CALLED JALEBI.

If you're from the UK you may not know what a funnel cake is – they haven't made their way across the pond just yet, and I'm not sure why. Traditionally made and eaten at amusement parks and fairgrounds up and down the US and Canada, there is something about this dessert that is a little bit dirty – in a good way. Nothing says childhood like eating mounds of hot, sweet, fried dough and then making yourself sick by going on loads of rollercoaster rides. So give it a go – rollercoasters optional.

MAKES ABOUT 4

1 tsp egg-replacement powder
1 tbsp lukewarm water

250g (2 cups) plain flour
60g (¼ cup + 1 tbsp) caster sugar
a pinch of salt

1 tsp baking powder
300ml (1¼ cups) soya or rice milk
½ tsp vanilla extract

light rapeseed or other flavourless oil, for deep-frying
icing sugar

Heat the oil in a deep-sided pan to about 180°C/350°F, or until a cube of bread dropped into the hot oil turns golden in 15 seconds. You need the oil to be at least 4cm (1½ inch) deep.

In a small bowl, whisk the egg-replacement powder with the tablespoon of lukewarm water until it is light and frothy.

In a separate bowl, mix together the flour, sugar, salt, and baking powder. Add the egg-replacement mixture and then the milk and vanilla until everything is just combined. The batter should be pourable, but not runny.

Pour a quarter of the batter into a cooking funnel, sealing the end with your finger to stop the batter running out. (If you don't have a funnel, use a measuring jug). Starting from the centre of the pan, drop the batter into the hot oil, moving outwards in a circular motion, keeping the circles of batter close together. Then go back over it in a crossways motion as if you are filling in the gaps. Fry for a couple of minutes and then turn the funnel cake over using tongs, to cook on the other side. Once golden brown, remove from the pan and blot with kitchen paper. Sprinkle with icing sugar and serve.

Dessert SANDWICHES

MAKE A SWEET QUESADILLA BY USING TORTILLAS INSTEAD OF SLICED BREAD.

As a lover of all things sweet (and fried), I've been making these dessert sandwiches for as long as I can remember. Bread makes an awesome dessert as it is brilliant at sucking up flavours and juices while still providing stability and texture. This dessert is also a great standby – you may not have flour in your cupboard, but I bet you've got a loaf of bread.

MAKES 1 SANDWICH

2 slices of bread

GLUTEN-FREE? Use gluten-free bread, biscuits and cereals.

dairy-free margarine,
 for spreading

1 x quantity Sandwich Filling
 (see next page)

icing sugar, to decorate (optional)

Leave the bread whole or use cutters to create different shapes. Spread one side of each slice with margarine. Place 1 slice, margarine-side down, on to a cold non-stick frying pan. Top with your chosen filling and place the other slice on top, margarine-side up.

Heat the pan to medium-high and fry the sandwich, pressing down lightly with a spatula to help seal the two sides together. After a couple of minutes, turn the sandwich over and cook until golden brown on both sides, flipping over as necessary. Remove from the pan and sprinkle with icing sugar if you like. Serve warm – but watch those melted fillings, they'll be hot!

Sandwich FILLINGS

PEANUT BUTTER AND BANANA

Spread the insides of both slices of bread with **peanut butter**, fill with thinly sliced **banana** and drizzle with **agave nectar**.

CRISPY PEANUT BUTTER FLUFF

Spread the insides of both slices of bread with **peanut butter** and fill with a small handful of **crisped rice cereal** and a few **vegan marshmallows**.

CHOCOLATE HAZELNUT

Mix 2 tablespoons of **cocoa powder** with 2 tablespoons of **agave syrup** and 1½ tablespoons **vegetable oil**. Leave in fridge to set for 30 minutes. Add 1 tablespoon of **crushed hazelnuts** and spread over the insides of your bread.

FRUITY TART

Spread the insides of both slices of bread with a small handful of **berries** (strawberries, blueberries, raspberries or blackberries) mixed with a heaped tablespoon of **fruit jam**.

CHOCOLATE MARSHMALLOW S'MORES

Fill your sandwich with a small handful of **dairy-free chocolate chips** (or 1 bar broken into small pieces), a few vegan **marshmallows** and 1 crushed **digestive biscuit**.

STRAWBERRY CHEESECAKE

Spread the insides of both slices of bread with **vegan cream cheese** and fill with a few roughly chopped, fresh **strawberries** mixed with 1 tablespoon of **strawberry jam**.

DEEP-FRIED *Chocolate* BARS

Now this is proper decadence. Our lovely Jayson (aka Veganbear) was the first to throw one of these in the fryer back when we first opened the shop. Deep-fried Chocolate Bars were apparently born up in Scotland in the early 1990s. No one said they were good for you back then, and even though we've put a vegan spin on them, I'm afraid they're still not good for you now! So proceed with caution.

MAKES 1 BAR

50g (scant ½ cup) plain flour
20g (4 tsp) caster sugar

a pinch of salt
½ tsp baking powder
30ml (2 tbsp) soya or rice milk

20ml (1 heaped tbsp) plain, vanilla or coconut soya yoghurt
½ tsp vanilla extract or essence

30g–50g (1–2oz) vegan chocolate bar
light rapeseed or vegetable oil, for deep-frying

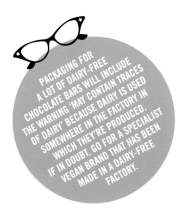

PACKAGING FOR A LOT OF DAIRY-FREE CHOCOLATE BARS WILL INCLUDE THE WARNING 'MAY CONTAIN TRACES OF DAIRY' BECAUSE DAIRY IS USED SOMEWHERE IN THE FACTORY IN WHICH THEY'RE PRODUCED. IF IN DOUBT, GO FOR A SPECIALIST VEGAN BRAND THAT HAS BEEN MADE IN A DAIRY-FREE FACTORY.

Heat the oil in a deep-sided pan, or deep-fat fryer, to about 180°C/350°F, or until a cube of bread dropped into the hot oil turns golden in 15 seconds.

In a large bowl, mix together the flour, sugar, salt and baking powder. Add the milk, yoghurt and vanilla and stir until fully combined – the mixture will be a bit gummy in texture.

Coat the chocolate bar in the batter making sure it's completely covered, then drop the bar into the hot oil. Fry until golden brown (about 2-3 minutes), turning with tongs as you go. When it is done, remove from the oil and allow to drain on a wire rack for a minute or two. Serve hot.

DEEP-FRIED *Cookie* DOUGH BALLS

Possibly the most bizarre recipe in the book, we discovered this by accident one day when we were making a batch of apple fritters and realised we didn't have any apples. What we did have in the fridge was some of our Chocolate-Chip Cookie dough. One thing led to another and we tried frying the cookie dough instead of chucking the batter away. Needless to say we were astounded by the results. Be careful to not fry for too long - you want the cookie dough to still be gooey and not quite cooked through when you bite into it.

MAKES ABOUT 10 BALLS

140g (1 cup + 1 tbsp) plain flour
60g (¼ cup + 1 tbsp) caster sugar
½ tsp salt
1½ tsp baking powder

90ml (⅓ cup + 2 tsp) soya or rice milk
50ml (¼ cup) plain, vanilla or coconut soya yoghurt
1 tsp vanilla extract or essence

1 x quantity Chocolate Chip Cookie dough (see page 102; Snickerdoodle or Peanut Butter Cookie dough – pages 113 and 107 – will also work)

light rapeseed or other flavourless oil, for frying
icing sugar, for dusting (optional)

IF YOU REALLY INSIST YOU COULD PROBABLY BAKE THE BATTERED BALLS INSTEAD OF FRYING THEM, BUT YOU'D END UP WITH A MORE COOKIE-LIKE CENTRE RATHER THAN AN OOZING, GOOEY ONE.

AS THE UNCOOKED DOUGH IS MADE WITHOUT EGGS, IT IS PERFECTLY SAFE TO EAT.

Heat the oil in a deep-sided pan, or deep-fat fryer, to 180°C/350°F/gas 4, or until a cube of bread dropped into the hot oil turns golden in 15 seconds.

In a large bowl, mix together the flour, sugar, salt and baking powder. Add the milk, yoghurt and vanilla and stir until fully combined – the mixture will be a bit gummy in texture.

Form 10 balls, each about 1 tablespoon in size, from the prepared cookie dough. Coat each one in the batter, making sure they are completely covered. Drop the coated balls one at a time into the hot oil. Fry them in small batches until golden brown (about 2–3 minutes), turning them as you go with tongs. When they are done, remove from the oil and transfer to a wire rack for minute or two to drain. Dust with icing sugar if you like and serve immediately.

EASY *Sweet* TREATS

Here's a selection of easy-to-assemble treats that are a great anytime 'pick-me-up'. They also make excellent handmade gifts - perfect for party bags. We've stuck some of them on sticks, but that's optional!

DECORATED MARSHMALLOWS

Skewer a marshmallow with a cocktail or cake-pop stick. Dip briefly into cold water and roll in colourful vegan sprinkles or coloured sugar. Set aside for a couple of hours to set.

CHOCOLATE DIPPED PRETZELS

Melt 5-parts chocolate and 1-part margarine together over a low heat. Dip your pretzels first in the chocolate mixture and then in some roughly chopped nuts (optional). Set aside until set.

CHOCOLATE DIPPED LIQUORICE CABLES

Melt 5-parts chocolate and 1-part margarine together over a low heat. Dip up to three-quarters of each liquorice cable into the chocolate mixture, then roll the chocolate end in sprinkles, chopped nuts or desiccated coconut. Set aside until set.

PEANUT BUTTER LUMPS (MAKES 5)

In a small pan over a medium heat, bring 2 tablespoons caster sugar and 2 tablespoons golden syrup to the boil, stirring frequently. Take the pan off the heat and stir in 2 tablespoons peanut butter until blended. Stir in 60 grams (1¾ cups) of cereal and a handful of chopped nuts. Set aside to cool for 2–3 minutes.

Coat the palms of your hands with margarine and shape about 2 tablespoons of the mixture into a ball. Immediately roll in sprinkles (if using). Repeat until you've used up all the mixture. Leave to set for about 15 minutes.

RUM BALLS

This one's super easy. All you need is some leftover chocolate cake.

Roll about 2 tablespoons of the cake in the palms of your hands to form balls. Dip into rum or rum flavouring and roll in cocoa powder. Continue until all the cake has been rolled into balls. Serve immediately.

NOT EVERYTHING YOU MAKE NEEDS TO START FROM SCRATCH. TRY LOOKING AT A SWEET PACK AND ASK YOURSELF 'HOW CAN I MAKE THIS EVEN BETTER?'

GLUTEN-FREE? Use gluten-free cereals, cake and candies.

UK Stockists AND Suppliers

The whole premise behind this book and our ethos as a company is that you should be able to get the majority of ingredients you need for the recipes from your local supermarket. However, if you live in a smaller town you may need to hunt a few things out online. Here is a guide to point you in the right direction.

If in London, please come visit us! We stock most of the sweets, treats and ingredients used in this book. You can find us at:

Ms. Cupcake
408 Coldharbour Lane
Brixton
London SW9 8LF

www.mscupcake.co.uk

THE FOLLOWING ONLINE RETAILERS AND BRANDS WILL HELP YOU BAKE YOUR WAY THROUGH THIS BOOK

Decorating Supplies and Food Colouring Pastes

www.squires-shop.com

www.hobbycraft.co.uk

www.cakecraftworld.co.uk

VEGAN SWEETS AND GROCERIES (DAIRY AND EGG REPLACEMENTS, JUNK FOOD, GLUTEN-FREE FLOURS ETC.)

www.veganstore.co.uk

www.vegancross.com

www.goodnessdirect.co.uk

Flavour Extracts and Essences

www.uncleroys.co.uk

Vegan Marshmallows

www.sweetvegan.co.uk

www.anandafoods.co.uk

Vegan Chocolate

www.moofreechocolates.com

www.plamilfoods.co.uk

VEGAN DAIRY REPLACEMENTS

Cream Cheese

www.buteisland.com

www.tofutti.com

Cream and Yoghurt

www.alpro.com

www.provamel.co.uk

shop.redwoodfoods.eu

BECOMING VEGAN

Interested in keeping your diet cruelty-free? Need advice avoiding ingredients you are allergic to? Try these UK-based folk for information and inspiration:

www.vegansociety.com

www.viva.org.uk

www.veggievision.tv

GOLDEN SYRUP
PERFECT FOR COOKING AND DRIZZLING

22806

CHEF'S LARDER

sea salt
For cooking and grinding
1kg e

Soja

Condensed
Soja
330g

Condensed
Soja
330g

SKIPPY

SKIPPY

SKIPPY

ACKNOWLEDGEMENTS

A ridiculous number of people have helped to build me and my business, and have watched this book come to life. I'd like to thank:

My Cupcake Crew (past and present). You have all helped to make my dreams a reality and I would be nowhere without you. Thank you – Sara, Fibi, Jhenn, Jemiamah, Tracy, Jayson, Alessio, Raquel, Tara, Ellie and Liz. Love also to honorary crew members Jojo, Kip, Bryan, Sean and Josh.

I also want to thank Karl, Russell, Greg, Ryan and Wendy, all of whom helped me to imagine the impossible in the beginning – I will always be thankful for that. Additionally I need to thank our customers who over the past 3 years have eaten up everything we have made. Thank you for your continued support.

Thank you to Rowan at Random House who had the crazy notion that I should write a book in the first place. Massive big-up for my editor Caroline and all at Square Peg and Random House, you are hugely patient, understanding and undyingly creative. It has been a dream working with you.

Thanks to Liz and Max Haarala Hamilton. You are the best photographers a gal could ever wish to work with. Your attention to detail is phenomenal and you are two of the loveliest people on the planet. Thanks also to Lucy, my amazing designer, who never gave up on me or my vision. Thank you for making this book look so beautiful.

Thank you to everyone at Limelight Management. If you hadn't taken a chance on a kooky lady like me, this book would never have happened. Also a huge thank you to David Powell for his continuing advice and mentorship.

Thanks to my crazy, ridiculous family, who have always let me be me. Mum, Dad, Melanie, Trish, Lina, Auntie D, Uncle Dyke, Tyler, Todd and Ryan – you taught me how to love and to always love with all your might – that has shaped me more than you will ever know. Also, a special shout out to the most incredible best friend a girl could ask for (that's you Pippa!). You have been there through it all, and you were always willing to listen.

Thank you to my rock and champion, Gareth. And a big final thank you to the light of my life – Jamie. I'm sorry Mummy works so much.

INDEX

MELLISSA MORGAN originally hails from Canada, but moved to the UK many moons ago. She started baking when she couldn't find indulgent bakery goods for vegans in London and soon realised that it wasn't just vegans that weren't being catering for. People allergic to foods like eggs and milk, and those who didn't eat certain things due to religious reasons were also missing out. Ms. Cupcake launched from Mellissa's home kitchen in the spring of 2010, selling vegan cakes at markets around London. She opened London's first entirely vegan retail bakery in Brixton in April 2011 and was named the Baking Industry Awards Rising Star of 2011 in September of that year. This is her first book.

Published by Square Peg 2013
10 9 8 7 6 5 4 3 2

Copyright © Mellissa Morgan

The Author has asserted her rights under the Copyright, Designs and Patents Act 1988 to be identified as the author of this work

Photography © Haarala Hamilton Photography

Thank you to Dupenny for permission to use their 'Time for Tea' wallpaper (page 24), available from www.dupenny.com

This book is sold subject to the condition that it shall not, by way of trade or otherwise, be lent, resold, hired out, or otherwise circulated without the publisher's prior consent in any form of binding or cover other than that in which it is published and without a similar condition, including this condition, being imposed on the subsequent purchaser

The Random House Group Limited Reg. No. 954009

Addresses for companies within The Random House Group Limited can be found at: www.randomhouse.co.uk

A CIP catalogue record for this book is available from the British Library

ISBN 978 0 22 409558 7

The Random House Group Limited supports the Forest Stewardship Council® (FSC®), the leading international forest-certification organisation. Our books carrying the FSC label are printed on FSC®-certified paper. FSC is the only forest-certification scheme supported by the leading environmental organisations, including Greenpeace. Our paper procurement policy can be found at www.randomhouse.co.uk/environment

Photography and styling: Haarala Hamilton
Design: Lucy Stephens
Home economist: Annie Rigg
Copy editor: Natasha Martyn-Johns
Proofreader: Imogen Fortes

Printed and bound in China by C&C Offset Printing Co., Ltd